The Last Year of Your Life

Personal Transformation Experience
2012 Special Edition
The Last Year Of The Mayan Calendar

by

CLINT ARTHUR

CLINT ARTHUR / I.C.S. Corporation
5348 Vegas Drive
Las Vegas, NV 89108
www.TheLastYearOfYourLife.com

Ordering Information:

Quantity sales. Special discounts are available on quantity purchases by corporations, associations, and others. For details, contact the publisher at the address above.

Orders by U.S. trade bookstores and wholesalers. Please contact Sales:
Tel: (702) 987-0113; Fax: (702) 938-8618 or visit www.TheLastYearOfYourLife.com

Printed in the United States of America

Publisher's Cataloging-in-Publication data
Arthur, Clint.
The Last Year Of Your Life / Clint Arthur.

ISBN 1453633642
1. Self Help 2. Spirituality 3. Inspirational

First Edition

CONTENTS

MONTH 7

Week 24. Align Yourself with Your Life's Purpose
Week 25. Give Yourself Permission to Have Fun Every Day
Week 26. Understand The True Foundation Of All Personal Power
Week 27. Appreciate Your Life Experience
Week 28. Flip A Switch to Create Real Courage to Change

MONTH 8

Week 29. Perfect Your Time Management Skills
Week 30. Access The Power Of What You Already Know
Week 31. Eliminate Your Fear Of Death
Week 32. Create Unstoppable Personal Power by Being Real
Week 33. Live A Life That's As Good As It Gets

MONTH 9

Week 34. Become A True Leader
Week 35. Get Passion In Your Life On A Cellular Level
Week 36. Understand and Access True Spirituality
Week 37. Experience "Joie de Vie" (The Joy Of Life)
Week 38. Take a Stand For Something Big In Your Life

MONTH 10

Week 39. Develop Genuine Connections with People
Week 40. Appreciate Each Moment of Your Life
Week 41. Unburden Yourself From Your Sins and Transgressions
Week 42. Make Amends to All People You Have Injured

MONTH 11

Week 43. Give Your "Last Lecture" & Become A Great Speaker
Week 44. Empower Yourself With Genuine Gratitude
Week 45. Resolve All Outstanding Personal Issues in Your Life
Week 46. Write Your Last Will and Testament
Week 47. Appreciate The Accomplishments of Your Entire Life

MONTH 12

Week 48. Understand the Meaning of Your Life
Week 49. Make Peace with Yourself and Your Higher Power
Week 50. Take Stock of Everything You Accomplished This Year
Week 51. Experience True Freedom
Week 52. Create A Clean Slate For The Rest of Your Life

PART 3: Create A Vision & Plan For Your Ideal Life in 5 Years Time

MY STORY

After I graduated from The Wharton Business School, I moved out to Los Angeles to pursue my dream of becoming a movie legend like my idol Spike Lee. After 10 years of chasing the Hollywood dream I found myself deep in credit card debt, driving a taxi to survive, and terrified I would never be able to turn my life around.

I started doing all kinds of self-help work to try and get my life going in a productive direction again. I walked on fire with Tony Robbins, I studied Toltec Wisdom with Don Miguel Ruiz. I did men's power circles, and continued in the Men's self-help movement as a participant and as a leader.

Things began to change for me. I started a gourmet food business and for the first time in my adult life actually enjoyed making money, I got married, I built 4 houses – and I became fat and happy. The only problem was that I had given up on my dreams of being a self-expressed creative person.

One night I was sitting in a men's self-help circle when a crippled old crazy man stood up from his chair, pointed a crooked claw at me, and said something that changed my life.

He said to me: "You don't know it yet, but you're already dead!"

I said to myself, *What the hell does that mean? What does he mean I'm already dead? You're already dead... You're already dead!*

I couldn't get that out of my mind.

It came to be New Year's Day and I sat down to write out my list of goals for the year, as I do on every New Year's Day, and that year I had a divine inspiration. I asked myself a question: *What would you want to do this year if this was going to be the last year of your life?*

That question inspired me and my whole circle of people in my life.

That year I lost forty pounds without changing my diet, joining a gym, or hiring a trainer.

That year I built a factory to produce the product I'd been buying from a manufacturer in another state. This was something I'd been procrastinating for five years, and if it weren't for that factory, my company would have gone out of business during The Great Recession.

That was the year I wrote my book about the lessons I learned at Wharton, which was something I had been procrastinating for ten years.

And most importantly, that year, with the help of my wife I was able to turn around my marriage—which had been experiencing some serious rough going at the 7-year mark—to the point where today, as I write this, we've been together 10 years, my wife and I both feel that our life together is better than ever, and our future together more promising than ever.

Other people who have lived The Last Year Of Your Life have also gotten amazing results. One man had been playing guitar and singing his whole life, but he had never recorded anything until The Last Year of Your Life Program, when he recorded an entire album of original music.

Another member, at the age of sixty-three (!), barely had two nickels to rub together when they started, but that year they wrote a business plan, found an investor, and opened a cupcake store in a major regional mall in Southern California. This summer their kids were working in the cupcake store! (How cool is that?!)

One of my favorite participants lost 42 pounds while he quit smoking, flew on an airplane for the first time in his life, and introduced his kids to their grandfather for the first time in their lives when he reconciled with his dad – whom he hadn't spoken to in 20 years!

And last summer, a woman fulfilled her dream of praying at her religion's holiest sites when she flew to the middle east and did just that for two weeks.

Along the way to achieving these tremendous milestones, members of the program practiced daily meditation and exercise; they expressed gratitude; they became healthier, happier, expanded their concept of what was possible, and treated their loved ones—and people they met in the street—with more respect and admiration than ever before.

Now how do you put a price on achieving a closer relationship with your God or higher power, with your spouse or your kids, achieving artistic or business aspirations? You can't – those are priceless results!

That's the difference between living The Last Year Of Your Life and having a bucket list. With a bucket list, you jump out of an airplane, you drive an Indy race car, and you fulfill a whole bunch of purely personal self-indulgent fantasy experiences so you don't feel like you missed out on anything. But with The Last Year Of Your Life you fulfill your hearts deepest longings and desires, you do things that are going to live beyond your lifetime, that are going to create a legacy.

Living The Last Year Of Your Life is one of the most exhilarating and rewarding experiences I've ever known, and I have designed this workbook to deliver the same results for you.

You can start on January first, or at any moment in time, and begin a personal journey in which you experience the Last Year of Your Life. Do it alone; or better yet, do it with a friend, coworker, colleague, or with family members. Men or women, young or old, the more the better—there's power in numbers! So try to put together a little group of people living the experience together, and you'll get even more out of it.

All that really matters is that you begin in earnest and live each day moving forward as if it is precious, and as if it were one of your last. Once you do this, your life will never be the same.

If you want to be part of an organized twelve-month online or live program, go to www.TheLastYearofYourLife.com and join the community of people all around the world who are living with a passion you can only get when you live as if you only have fifty-two weeks left on this Earth.

I dedicate this book to your success, fulfillment, and the greatness of your own life, and I salute you for having the courage to really go for it!

Sincerely, *Clint Arthur*

How to Get the Most from This Experience

First of all, I want you to trust me. From here on out, believe that I am your friend, I want the best for you, and everything I'm going to ask of you is intended to help you get the most you possibly can from The Last Year of Your Life.

This will be your very own personal action guide for The Last Year of Your Life. Write in it! Fill in all the blanks! Do all the Action Items and the exercises; make notes in the margins; doodle in blank spaces; record your feelings, emotions, hopes, dreams, fears, and random thoughts. It is yours, and I want you to fully personalize it.

I have a feeling that you will pull out this book many times over the years to come—once you have been reborn and are living your new life—and will look back fondly over the twelve months of this intense experience you are creating for yourself. So use the book!

DO NOT SKIP AHEAD. I want you to be like a wide-eyed little kid and let me lead you through the adventure. Allow yourself the luxury of being surprised by what comes next.

Get a partner or "buddy" to go through this experience with you – and this way you can both hold each other accountable and share the process. It will be amazing for you, and really bond you two together. Do it with your spouse or significant other and watch your relationship deepen ten levels.

Most of all, enjoy the **process** of The Last Year of Your Life. Enjoy the discovery…the emotions…the unknown.

Remember: A warrior thrives under any and all circumstances. In The Last Year of Your Life, you are the warrior, and you are on a sacred crusade to get the very most out of every single moment.

There are fewer moments left in this experience than you think. Enjoy each and every one!

Week 1. Really Feel Unconditional Love For Yourself

"Self–love, my liege, is not so vile a sin, as self–neglecting."
–William Shakespeare

I grew up in New York City and I got my first job at the age of eleven, handing out flyers on street corners. The wage: a whopping one dollar an hour. But that was enough to get me hooked on money.

I loved making money. Whenever I got any money, whether it be from handing out flyers, delivering flowers or dry cleaning, birthday gifts from aunts or grandparents, or from the tooth fairy, I would come home from elementary school during lunch break and deposit that money in my Chase Manhattan Bank savings account. Then I'd go upstairs to our apartment on the eighteenth floor and daydream over the steadily growing balance in my passbook: $3.29...$4.38...$6.49...$11.01. I loved it.

When I was fourteen years old I read about the Wharton Business School, "The best business school in the world." I was intrigued by this idea of going to a college where you studied making money, and I looked it up in the encyclopedia to make sure it was real. (Yes, back in those days we had a whole set of encyclopedias up on the bookshelf.)

Wharton was a real place—the place where captains of industry were trained in the fine art and science of business. This was amazing to me, and inspirational, and at that very moment—at the age of fourteen—I made up my mind that I was going to attend the world-famous Wharton Business School.

Despite the fact that I came from a normal, middle-class family with no connections and no buildings on campus named after my father or uncle or anybody I knew, I did attend and graduate from Wharton. I earned a 4.0 GPA in my Entrepreneurial Management business concentration—the study of how to run your own business.

I led a storybook life until that point, but then something weird happened. I got an offer to work on Wall Street with an investment banking firm—which was the career choice most in vogue at Wharton in the 1980s—but instead of accepting, I decided to go to Italy, buy a motorcycle, become a painter, and sell my paintings on the street.

This turned out not to be the cleverest career decision a Wharton man ever made. One thing led to another, and by the time I was thirty-five years old I had been driving taxi cabs and "pirate" taxis for five years.

As you could imagine, after graduating from the best business school in the world and spending five years as a taxi driver, I wasn't loving myself very much. A reflection of this lack of self-love was my idea of an exciting dinner in those days: a ninety-nine cent Whopper Jr. and three or four bottles of Miller Lite. Seriously.

But then another weird thing happened. I injured my knees, and I could barely walk. I literally had to use both hands to support my weight on the banisters as I went down a flight of stairs. It was scary to be a young man who was practically too crippled to walk down a flight of stairs.

One day my chiropractor suggested that I try to heal my body using raw nutrition, and he pointed me towards a book about the Raw Primal Diet called We Want to Live Free From Disease. According to that book, the remedy for my weak legs that felt like they were going to give out from under me was to eat lots of raw oysters, clams, and scallops—my favorite foods.

The idea of eating lots of raw oysters, clams, and scallops really excited me, and I jumped into the raw primal lifestyle with both feet. Soon my idea of an exciting dinner had become raw oysters and clams, thin-sliced raw steak (from Whole Foods market) sprinkled with raw cheeses, olives, and extra-virgin olive oil, along with a nice bottle of wine and slices of fresh fruit for dessert.

Do you see the difference in the signal this meal sends to a person's subconscious mind about how much that person loves oneself, as compared to the Whopper Jr. meal?

I didn't understand everything that was going on at the time, but within six months I was able to go out dancing again. And within a year (by January of 2001) I had quit the taxi racket and had become an entrepreneur in the food business making more than fifteen hundred dollars a week in cash.

Then one more very interesting thing happened that helped me to stop mentally beating myself up and love myself more. You recall that I had turned down a job offer from an investment bank in New York...that firm was located on the 87th floor of 1 World Trade Center.

As I watched the tragic events of September 11th unfold on television, I slowly began to realize that there might be a bigger plan for my life than working on Wall Street. Somehow, against all odds, I had been guided by an invisible hand that turned me away from my path with the herd of my fellow Wharton classmates and led me instead onto a completely different and totally unique path.

Ever since then, the events of my life have unfolded to reveal a date with destiny that I've had to become a leader in my life, to become an innovator, to learn all the varied skills and lessons that were required to create The Last Year of Your Life Program, and to write this book.

After everything that I've been through, I can say unequivocally that everything starts with loving yourself. It is the key to everything: success, happiness, fulfillment, and all relationships. Everything.

Unless you love yourself first, you cannot get anywhere in life.

What follows are some very simple things you can do to jump-start the process of loving yourself more.

A) Eat Well

The better food you feed yourself, the more your body knows that you love yourself.

Think about your car. Would you ever pour a Coca-Cola into your gas tank? That's an extreme example, but I hope you get the point. You wouldn't even use diluted gasoline. You only put the correct fuel in your engine because you know it would get ruined otherwise.

The same goes for your body. The only difference is that the human body has a lot more tolerance for variety in fuel than most engines do. You can eat paper, plastic, dirt—even glass!—and survive. But you can't thrive, physically or emotionally, if you feed your body a steady diet of rubble.

Feeding your body good organic foods, especially healthful foods that you love, will give your body the good fuel it wants and give your soul a message that you love yourself.

During The Last Year of Your Life, I want you to eat every meal like it's one of your very last. Eat the foods you love. And eat the very best of each kind of food that you can get your hands on.

Treat every meal as though it's a celebration of your life. I want you to be excited to eat your food because it looks and smells so great. I want you to present it to yourself in the best and most attractive way you possibly can. And I want you to take your time enjoying each and every healthful, loving bite.

Bon appetite!

B) Look Your Best

You look the way you feel, and the opposite is also true: you feel the way you look. So put extra effort into looking good every single day.

Personal grooming is not just to impress your mom, your boss, or members of the opposite sex. It's also a key signal to yourself that you love yourself.

When the person staring back at you in the mirror looks like a million bucks, it makes you feel great! Conversely, when you look like a mess, it sure doesn't help you to feel much better than that.

Good grooming and dressing well are very clear signals to yourself that you respect and love yourself.

When you see a well-dressed and put-together person in a magazine or walking down the street, you feel some admiration for that person. (Admit it, you do!) The same holds true when you see yourself dressed well and all put together in a photo or in a mirror.

Self-admiration is a great way to improve the amount of self-love you have. So make an effort to look your best and dress well every single day during The Last Year of Your Life.

Get rid of your torn and ratty clothes. Get a great haircut and buy your favorite soap, shampoo, conditioners, and other grooming products. Put yourself together every single day as though you were going out on a job interview or audition.

But keep in mind, The Last Year of Your Life is not a dress rehearsal—it's your final 365 days. So look your best for every single one of them.

C) Be Physically Fit

You cannot feel great and love yourself fully unless your body is working properly. The surest way to have your body work well is to maintain its proper ability to function. This can only be done with exercise.

Everyone knows that if you just let a machine sit on a shelf collecting dust, after a time it will begin to degrade and break down from lack of use! This is exactly why you have to use your body.

If you are so out of shape that you can only start with a short walk around the block, then that's how you have to start. (That's exactly what I did when I began to shed forty-five pounds and get down from 236 to 195 last year.) Walk. Every day.

You know that exercise makes you feel great—even exhilarated! So give yourself that gift of love. Being able to move allows you to do more things in life and helps reinforce the message of love you will feel by looking your best.

D) Be Loving to Yourself

Do things you love to do. You only have 364 more days to do stuff that you enjoy, so go for it!

If you like going to the movies, then go to the Chinese Theater or Radio City and see a great movie on a huge screen with amazing sound!

NASCAR? Get to the Indy 500 and f-e-e-l the roar of those engines!

Are you a foodie? Go to Le Cirque at Bellagio and taste some of their incredible, edible creations. Or get to a farmer's market and buy the most amazing ingredients you can find to prepare yourself a feast today!

Listen to music that you love whenever you can.

Drive places using your favorite route.

Wear your favorite clothes, use your best china, pull out the good jewelry, have the car detailed (and get all the dents fixed), buy yourself a present, go out for ice cream, go to the Louvre, or make time to attend your kid's school play.

Whatever it is that you love, you must make time to do it as much as you can this year.

Have the very best time you possibly can this year, doing all the things that you love to do most. Because you deserve it.

ACTION ITEMS:

List twelve things that you love to do, and do one each month:

1.   7.

2.   8.

3.   9.

4.   10.

5.   11.

6.   12.

List your seven favorite foods:

1.

2.

3.

4.

5.

6.

7.

Eat each of these foods this week, and eat them as much as you can all during this last year of your life.

List your favorite musicians, artists, and performers:

1.	6.
2.	7.
3.	8.
4.	9.
5.	10.

Actively seek out the work of these artists that you love and bring it into your daily life. Play the music at work and at home. Put pictures by the artists up on your computer screensaver. Go see concerts, comedy performances, and watch television shows. During The Last Year of Your Life, do whatever you can to feed your soul with the loving artistry that really fires you up.

List ten things that you love about yourself:

1.

2.

3.

4.

5.

6.

7.

8.

9.

10.

List five things that you love about yourself that you don't think are really virtuous, but you love yourself for doing them anyway.

(This is a tough one. For example, when I'm not with a person, I don't usually miss them. If you are not with me, then I am most likely not even thinking about you! I love myself for being so present in the moment, but I don't think it's my most admirable quality. Sometimes I really feel bad about it and that I shouldn't love myself for this quality. But I do. ;)

1.

2.

3.

4.

5.

Week 2. Acknowledge Your Greatness

"It is not the mountain we conquer but ourselves."
–Edmund Hillary

We are going to continue building on the huge stuff we did last week by focusing on how great a person you are and all the things you have accomplished in your life so far.

Most of us get a lot of input from the world around us about what terrible, tiny, inconsequential people we've been, but we don't have a lot of people telling us that we are great. So we tend to forget.

This week I want you to think about all the things you have accomplished in your life, and acknowledge yourself for them.

Keep in mind that just surviving is an accomplishment—especially these days!

Having the guts to take on The Last Year of Your Life program is a huge feat as well!

Falling in love is an act of courage worthy of acknowledgement.

Graduating from high school, college, technical school, basic training, and getting a GED are all great things too!

Are you a good dancer, a great cook, artist, mother or father, son or daughter, brother or sister, or friend?

Being a good friend to someone in need is something that is definitely worthy of acknowledgement from yourself.

Let's get right into action on this…

List ten things you achieved as a kid:

1.

2.

3.

4.

5.

6.

7.

8.

9.

10.

List ten things you've achieved as an adult:

1.

2.

3.

4.

5.

6.

7.

8.

9.

10.

Okay, now I want you to take a little bit of a risk and get together with someone who knows you. A spouse, relative, or old friend would be best. Tell them about The Last Year of Your Life program and that you want to do an exercise with them. Ask their permission to get personal with them, and when they agree, do this:

ACTION ITEM:

Tell your exercise partner at least five things that they have accomplished in their life that you really think they deserve acknowledgement for. Tell them, "I want to acknowledge you for..."

1.

2.

3.

4.

5.

Now, ask them to tell you five or more things that they think you have accomplished in your life that are worthy of acknowledgement. Hopefully they will tell you things that you didn't think of yourself in the work you did earlier in this section.

When it's over, thank them for helping you with this project, write their name on the blank line below, and then write down the things they acknowledged you for below.

The five things that _____ acknowledged me for:

1.

2.

3.

4.

5.

Now here's the tough one: Acknowledge two mistakes that you've made in your life and the lessons you learned from them.

MISTAKE 1:

LESSON 1:

MISTAKE 2:

LESSON 2:

Week 3. Create A Plan That Gets You Jumping Out Of Bed Every Morning With Your Blood Pumping & Feeling Lust for Life

"Good fortune is what happens when opportunity meets with planning."
– Thomas Alva Edison

Now I'm going to teach you some seriously powerful technology that I learned in the Men's Division. It's called CPR, and it stands for Context, Purpose, Results.

We use CPRs all the time on the men's teams. My wife and I use them in "real life" too—we each write a CPR for the year (since 2003,) and we've done CPR work with groups and friends (both men and women) over the years. It's awesomely powerful, and here's how it works:

Let's say, for example, you want to make a plan for The Last Year of Your Life so that you are sure to get the most out of the experience. The first thing you need to do is write down a list of the Results you want to get. That's the R in CPR.

There are two kinds of results: concrete and ethereal.

Concrete results are very precise, measurable, black–and–white. You know if you got the concrete result because it is very specific. Examples of concrete results are:

• I lost twenty–five pounds.

• I visited Paris for one week and Madrid for ten days.

• I took a three–week vacation at a tropical resort with my spouse.

- I bought myself a new hybrid vehicle.

- I wrote the first draft of my mystery novel.

- I went fishing once a month with my kids.

- I took a forty-five minute walk every day.

- I ate three meals each day.

- I completed The Last Year of Your Life Program, including all the Exercises and Action Items.

- I participated in a real Native American sweat lodge.

- I set up a life insurance policy for my wife and kids.

- I saw one more great concert.

Results are always stated in the past tense, and you'll see why later.

At the end of the year, when you inspect your results, with the concrete results you either got 'em or you didn't, and you'll be able to check off the ones you got very easily.

Ethereal results are more conceptual, not so easy to inspect, and harder to attain. Examples of ethereal results are:

- I developed a closer relationship with God.

- I did everything possible to improve my marriage.

- I was a loving, kind, and supportive father.

- I developed a circle of trusting friends and mentors.

- I co-created a fulfilling, honest, and elevating relationship with the future mother of my child.

- I mastered my job.

- I was a great example for my children.

• I created peace in my life.

• I helped my boys become the men they want to be.

• I took time whenever I could to smell the roses.

As you can see, there are some really amazing ethereal results you can set for yourself, but they are a lot harder to check off as "accomplished."

I suggest creating a good mix of concrete and ethereal results for yourself. The more you have, the more you will accomplish during The Last Year of Your Life. You will be absolutely amazed at how your subconscious mind will go about accomplishing results without you even having to think about it.

On one of my annual CPR's I wrote, "Achieved page one Google rank for three search terms" and I got it! I didn't even say to myself, "Okay, this week I'm going to get those page one Google rankings." It just naturally happened as a course of normal business activities, and at the end of the year when I was reviewing my results I was surprised to have gotten that one.

You can add to or delete results from your list as you progress through the year—it's The Last Year of Your Life, after all.

Realistic vs. Pie in the Sky:

There is something to be said about shooting for the moon. One participant of the program last year wrote the result "I viewed Earth from outer space."

On the other hand, there's a lot to be said about knowing your own limitations and setting goals for yourself that you can actually achieve.

To me, it feels a lot more satisfying to achieve my results than to set myself up for failure. What I like to do is write a list of results that seem just a bit beyond my reach — results which will definitely make me stretch and grow, but ones I can actually get, here on this planet, in this lifetime.

ACTION ITEM:

Write down at least ten concrete results and ten ethereal results for you to achieve during The Last Year of Your Life: (Imagine yourself in 11½ months having already accomplished these results over the course of this year.)

CONCRETE RESULTS:

1.

2.

3.

4.

5.

6.

7.

8.

9.

10.

ETHEREAL RESULTS:

1.

2.

3.

4.

5.

6.

7.

8.

9.

10.

Good Job! Especially if you wrote more than ten concrete results!

Now let's move on to the C in CPR: context. Context is like a T-shirt that you wear which silently announces what you're all about to everyone you encounter—without you ever having to say a word.

The context is also what will get you out of bed in the morning.

If you change your context, you change your world. Until you started The Last Year Of Your Life, you most likely had no conscious context for your life, or your life was running on a very low-level context like "I'm going to work each day to earn a living." Not very inspirational or energizing.

For the purposes of this experience, you and I have agreed on the context: The Last Year of Your Life. Do you feel the difference? Do you feel more urgency and power in your life with that as your context? That is the power of context.

Lastly, let's examine the P in CPR: Purpose. What is the purpose of your CPR for The Last Year of Your Life? When you look back over the whole of the year, what do you want to be able to say about it? Here are some examples from prior participants:

"To finally break free of limiting beliefs and live with a sense of personal joy and freedom."

"To become the man I have always wanted to be: self-reliant, rich, kind, generous, understanding, beloved by myself and my loved ones."

"To live a full life, surrounded by love, so that I can fully embrace my death knowing that I have been pushed and constantly seeking to improve myself and grow."

"To live and enjoy life to the fullest capacity at all times so that I can give love and be in love every moment."

"To awaken the deepest gratitude for the life I've lived, so that those around me connect with the joy of each moment, and profoundly understand the perfection of both life and death."

"To live with love and service for myself and all people I meet."

"To create passion by sharing, loving and giving, for myself and all whom I contact."

ACTION ITEM:

What is the purpose of The Last Year of Your Life?

_____

_____

_____

_____

Okay, you are almost done with this section, and all you have left is to consolidate and refine your CPR on the following page. This will be your plan for the Last Year of Your Life. Do your best! And when you're done, sign your name on the bottom line.

Turn the page and get to it!

NOTE: At the bottom of the next page you will see a place for you to sign your CPR and the numbers 1 – 12 below it. Each month you are to re-read your CPR and INITIAL one of the 12 numbers, so that you know you have done it every month and can inspect yourself that way.

CONTEXT: The Last Year of My Life

PURPOSE:_____

_____

RESULTS: It is write the date 365 days from the start of your adventure**, and I...**

1.

2.

3.

4.

5.

6.

7.

8.

9.

10.

11.

12.

13.

14.

15.

16.

17.

18.

19.

20.

s i g n a t u r e

_____

| 1 | 2 | 3 | 4 | 5 | 6 | 7 | 8 | 9 | 10 | 11 | 12 |

DRAW SOMETHING HERE....

Week 4. Amplify Your Personal Power by Being "All In"

"All that is necessary to break the spell of inertia and frustration is this:
Act as if it were impossible to fail. That is the talisman, the formula,
the command of right–about–face which turns us from failure towards success."
–Dorthea Bragg

Now that you've been involved with this program for almost a month, I expect that you've seen some changes occurring in your life.

Is it easier to get out of bed in the morning?

Are you having more meaningful interactions with people?

Are your conversations getting deeper, and are you probing under the surface with people?

Are you wasting less time on B.S.?

Are you having more fun in your life?

Have you made any significant discoveries about yourself? About what you really like or dislike? About what you are willing to invest your precious time on?

Are you showing up just the same as you always have, or has something shifted?

ACTION ITEMS

1) Write down three things about your life now that are different than before you started The Last Year of Your Life:

     1.

     2.

     3.

2) Off the top of your head, write down one place where you would like to see something change in your life, and what that change would look like in an ideal world:

The single most important change I want for my life would be:

_____

If you filled in the blanks above, then good job!

If you haven't, stop right here and FILL IN THOSE BLANKS! (I'm serious!)

Okay, now I want you to look at that last blank you filled in and think about it for a minute or two while considering this question: How awesome would it be to get that change for myself?

Would that change your entire life?

What would that change be worth to you?

I want a change for you that would forever transform your life; a change that would inspire you; a change that would be a complete point of departure for you. I want you to say, "There was life before I _____, and after that, my life was forever different."

For me, that change happened at the end of 2000 when I stopped being a taxi driver.

For a little over five years I earned my living by driving a cab on Friday and Saturday nights. On New Year's Eve of the millennium, I was driving a cab. It felt like shit to know that everyone in the whole world was out partying and celebrating, while I was driving a taxi.

I was so afraid I was never going to get out of the rut I had dug for myself that I started taking major transformative seminars: Paul Roth's "Life Transformation," "The Sterling Men's Weekend," and finally "Unleash the Power Within" with Tony Robbins.

In December of 2000, if someone had asked me "What is the single most important change you want to make in your life?" I would have instantly answered, "I don't want to be a cab driver anymore!"

I'm willing to bet that there's something churning inside you like that—some secret dream or dread that you've been trying (unsuccessfully) to ignore for months, or even years!

Did you write that down in that blank? If not, WRITE IT DOWN NOW!

I want something very specific from you. I want a commitment to something that you are willing to go "All In" for. Your last stand. All your chips pushed into the pot. Something you are willing to lay your life on the line for, if necessary.

Come on, have the courage to make a stand for something that inspires you!

Now here's the really tough part: You have to take a leap of faith with me—a leap of faith that you won't let yourself down. That you won't fall into the deep dark chasm...that you won't plunge yourself onto a spear...that you won't embarrass yourself to death.

You see, here's the thing about The Last Year of Your Life: I'm going to ask you to take yourself on a journey unlike anything you've ever participated in before.

We are going into the deep dark unknown. We are going to plumb the depths of your psyche and your soul.

We are going to test your endurance, your commitment, your creativity, your courage, your trust, your integrity, your spiritual base, your ability to deal with people, your ability to persevere in the face of the unknown, and even your ability to face death—to look it square in the eye and triumph.

And I want you to make a commitment to yourself—right now—that you are willing to do everything that I ask you to do, from here on out, all the way to the very last moment of The Last Year of Your Life. This is your commitment:

"I will do all the Action Items. I will do all the Exercises. I will do everything in The Last Year of Your Life Program, fully and to the very best of my ability... Because I want more out my life than I've experienced so far... Because I want to live my life to the absolute peak of my potential.... Because I believe in **myself** and my own **courage** and my ability to **succeed** and be the **best me that I can be**."

If you can't make this commitment right here, right now, and forevermore so help you God, then I want you to close this book, take it back to where you got it, and hand it in for a full refund.

I only want fully all-in participants from here on out. I want people who are committed to achieving life-transforming results in this program. I only want people who are 100 percent committed to changing their lives for the better—to becoming the men or women they have always wanted to be.

The Last Year of Your Life is a program exclusively for gutsy, 100 percent committed winners who are willing to do whatever it takes to achieve their personal ideals. If that's not you, then it's been nice knowing you, thanks for giving this a try, and I wish you the best of luck. You will receive your refund with all politeness.

But if that is you... Then read the statement below aloud, write today's date, and then sign your name on the dotted line:

"I am 100 percent committed to live The Final Year of My Life to the fullest. I am ALL IN!"

_____	_____
date	signature

To those of you who read the statement aloud and signed your name, I say, "Congratulations! I look forward to meeting you personally, and I eagerly await the moment when I hear your stories about your greatness!"

Sincerely,

Clint Arthur

What it really means to live The Last Year of Your Life

I had a conversation today with a participant in the program. This is a woman who has not had a job in over three years and is eating through her savings. She has formerly been paid more than $200,000 a year in a very high-profile job.

In our conversation last night I advised her to get a job. I told her that in order to get her income flowing again—she has aspirations of having $20,000 a month in income—she has to get it started with something before she can begin doubling and tripling it. It's been my experience that it's very hard to go from zero income to $20,000 a month.

So I lectured her very sternly about how important it was for her to get her ego out of her way and just get a job. She doesn't want to go backwards on the career ladder, even though she's getting older and the jobs in her field aren't generally available for a person of her age.

In fact, after we concluded our conversation, I called her back intending to lecture her even more strenuously about how important it was for her to get a job, but she didn't answer the phone because it had gotten late and she had gone to sleep.

Today, early in the morning I got a text message from her saying to please call, and I did. What she said was very instructive for me.

She said, "Look, this is The Last Year of My Life. Getting a job is not going to fulfill me, especially during The Last Year of My Life. If this is The Last Year of My Life, I want to pursue my dreams. And while I still have the money, I'm going to do it."

I thought about this and I really took it in.

This is The Last Year of Your Life, and I think now, having had this conversation with that participant, I believe in my responsibility to inspire people to go for their dreams more than ever before. So I've totally changed my mind with that woman.

I believe she should not get a job. I believe she should go for it. I believe she should pursue her dream, and I've encouraged her to go for it 100 percent—with the caveat, though, that if she doesn't make it happen by the end of this last year of her life, that she has to be open to the possibility that when she's reborn she will go out and get a job.

But in the meantime, I encourage her and I encourage everyone else to say "Fuck it! This is The Last Year of My Life, and I'm pursuing my dreams with everything I have, with every breath in my body, with every ounce of my energy, and with every fiber in my soul."

*****

She called and shared this dream with me the very next day:

"I dreamt I was going on a plane. I was driving a truck going to the airport, and I had obstacles in my way of getting on that plane. I dropped my friends off at the airport, they were already on the plane; they were drinking cocktails, waiting for me on the plane.

I parked the car. I didn't have the right suitcase; I didn't have my coat; it was one excuse after another, then I had the wrong suitcase, and then I didn't get there in time so I couldn't check my bag in, and then I parked in a handicap zone and I was going to get a ticket, and an alarm was going off…

And the entire time there was a little girl that was with me, ten or eleven years old, and she kept saying, "Come on, let's go, you've got your suitcase, we'll check it in when we get to the plane."

And I said, "But I don't have a coat."

She said, "Don't worry; we'll get you a coat."

"But I parked in the handicap zone."

"Don't worry; an alarm's just going to go off, that's all. It's all going to be good."

Then we were walking through a cheese store as a shortcut to get to the gate (we were still at the airport) and this time it was me saying, "Hurry up, I don't want to miss that plane, hurry up! Stop eating cheese!" She kept sampling all the cheeses along the way, and I kept saying, "Hurry up!"

Then I stopped and picked up a little sample of cheese and it had tortilla chips in it, and she asked me what I had, and I said it was cheese with tortillas in it, and it was really good.

Then she looked at me again and said, "Don't worry. There is nothing that is going to stop you from getting on that plane."

"The end."

Is that not awesome?

Week 5. Create Inner Peace by Forgiving Yourself

Rembrandt "The Return of The Prodigal Son"

"To forgive is the highest, most beautiful form of love.
In return, you will receive untold peace and happiness."
–Robert Muller

We have all made mistakes in the course of being alive. Some of them have been huge, and we continue to beat ourselves up over them in our internal chatter—holding lists on ourselves, being bitter, angry, and disappointed.

In order to move forward with a fresh and open perspective, we've got to expose those old wounds to the light of day so that they can be worked out and healed.

When I was a kid in high school, I got into wrestling on the varsity team. My first year on the team was a constant stream of demoralizing defeats and public humiliations. But the whole team went to wrestling camp for one week during summer vacation, and we lifted weights, we listened to our coaches (especially Coach Mike Ognibene), and we became a great team during my senior year.

We competed in the Manhattan and Bronx Division of the New York City Public School Athletic League, so most of our matches required us to travel up to Harlem and the Bronx by subway. We were a bunch of skinny white and Asian kids wrestling against murderers and other assorted criminals in the Bronx and Harlem, but we had technical skill, we trained hard, and we had a lot of heart, so we won and won and won.

In fact, nobody beat us all year long, and we found ourselves wrestling for the PSAL gold medal one cold January afternoon in 1983.

Wrestling matches are scored on a point system. The maximum points a wrestler can score for his team is six, which is awarded when a wrestler pins his opponent during a match. This six-point maximum is also awarded if a wrestler is disqualified for using any illegal move which results in his opponent being unable to continue the match.

So there I was, wrestling the captain of the other team—a guy who was a former New York City Wrestling gold medalist and a Judo champion. To top it all off, he looked to me like he was crazed out of his mind with bloodlust.

He came after me like a Tasmanian devil right in the beginning of the match, picked me up, and simply chucked my whole body twelve feet across the mat.

I landed on my ass, wide-eyed with disbelief, shocked at his crazed behavior, and bewildered as to what I was going to do in order to subdue this beast. My mind was racing, and I was panicked between thoughts of getting humiliated, of whether I could I possibly match physicality with him, and of whether I could hold up against his irrational brute force.

Luckily, just a moment later, the referee blew his whistle and called that maniac for an illegal move, thus stopping the clock.

The whole auditorium full of four hundred people got silent.

I collapsed flat onto the mat and laid there breathing calmly, staring at the lights on the ceiling some thirty feet above, until Doug Palczewski, the head coach of my team sauntered over to me.
Coach Palczewski stood there looking down at me on the floor, barely able to control his shit-eating grin, because he knew what was going to happen.

Above all, we were a great wrestling team because we outsmarted our opponents, and here was an opportunity for an easy six points at a crucial moment in the match.

Coach said, "How you feeling?"

A dozen thoughts flashed through my mind in about two seconds. Can I beat this guy? Will he pin me? Am I going to get humiliated in front of the pretty girls from my school? Is this guy going to hurt me? Could I possibly pin him? What's the right thing to do? What's the smart thing to do? How scared am I? Am I a coward?

I said, "Not good, Coach."

He shook his head and grinned. "Just lay there."

Then he walked back to the bench and left me staring at the lights on the auditorium ceiling for a few minutes before he returned with a couple of my teammates, who helped me to my feet. I put my arms around their shoulders and limped off the mat, trying not to ham it up too much.

The referee awarded us six points for the disqualification of my opponent, and my team went on to win the New York City Public School Athletic League Wrestling Team Championship with a margin of victory of one point.

I have no doubt in my mind that my decision not to continue that match was the "right" decision for the team, and most likely for my own vanity at the time—there was a good chance that guy was going to hurt and/or humiliate me that day.

But little did I know what the psychic toll of that decision would be, and how I would continue to pay a price for that moment of cowardice, doubt, and weakness in the years to come.

By my junior year of college I started to feel a lack of willingness to compete when, one afternoon, I was riding my bike to campus and refused to race against some guy who rode up beside me.

This lack of desire got more and more acute as I got older, as things didn't go my way more and more, and as competition for everything seemed to intensify.

Around the age of thirty-five I began self-help work with a life coach named Paul Roth, and through that work I came to realize the impact of that crisis decision I'd made some fourteen years earlier. I began the long process of forgiving myself for my moment of weakness.

Forgiveness is not easy—especially when it comes to forgiving ourselves, because we know the truth behind everything that happened. We know what a lousy, tiny, craven, wicked, evil person really dwells inside each of us.

And let's face it; there's a perverse thrill in knowing we're right about our own self-condemnation. It feels good to be right, even if you're being right about the fact that you are just a piece of crap!

But this kind of certitude comes with the highest price of anything.

This kind of rightness will keep a person stuck for decades.

This is a toll that will bankrupt a person's soul, and nobody can afford to pay that price forever.

Somewhere in your history is your own personal Waterloo—your moment of weakness, failure, corruption, disgrace, etc., and you know exactly where it is because you've been thinking about it this whole time. And you've been worried that I was going to call you on it and make you drudge up the pain...

And you were right.

ACTION ITEMS:

1) Write down your most shameful, horrible, weakest moment of your life.

_____

_____

Congratulations, you're finished with the easy part.

2) Get together with a friend or a stranger and confess these transgressions against your soul to that other person. Tell them everything you can remember about why you did what you did, how you did it, when, where, and most importantly, how you feel about it now.

3) Take a long walk by yourself on the beach, or in the woods, or in the mountains, and think about how you have sold out yourself in your moments of weakness that you are dealing with now. If you can possibly cry about it, please cry about it.

And then when you are all done, you need to forgive yourself. Scream it out loud! "I FORGIVE MYSELF FOR_____!"

4) For the next month, I want you to start every single day by looking in the mirror before you brush your teeth and saying aloud, "I forgive myself for [whatever you did], and I love myself enough to let it go."

Do another drawing here, or paste in a collage
about how you feel right now.

Week 6. Train Your Brain for Success

"All that we are is the result of what we have thought."
– Buddha

Human beings think an average of 65,000 thoughts per day, and 85 percent of them are the exact same thoughts you had the day before.

Day after day, you spend most of your time thinking the same thoughts you thought the day before.

This means that you are essentially a robot, repeating the same thousands of thought-patterns day after day after day. And what we think about, we become. This is why most people's lives never change.

To compound the issue, 95 percent of your thoughts occur on a subconscious level—meaning you have no active control over them, because they are automatic tape-loops playing in your brain.

An example of subconscious thinking would be your ability to get in your car and drive to work or the supermarket without even thinking about it. How many times have you gotten out of your car at your destination only to think to yourself, "Wow, I don't even remember driving here!"

When we were little children we soaked up the information coming at us like super-absorbent sponges, and the place in the brain where all those opinions, attitudes, emotions, and beliefs reside—to this very day—is in the subconscious.

All those times that your uncle told you that you were not so pretty—that opinion of you lives on in your subconscious mind, echoing in your thoughts, day after day.

All those times that your grandmother said you were a klutz, or not so smart, or not as well-behaved as your brother or your cousin or your mother when she was a kid—all of that keeps repeating in your subconscious mind as part of those 55,250 thoughts that are reruns from the previous day's hit parade.

Having studied this subject with Robert Irwin, Ph.D., as part of his Train Your Brain for Success program, I had the privilege of being the guinea pig who stood up in front of the class and got worked on.

"What is the result you're getting in your life that you're not happy about?" Doctor Irwin asked me.

I said, "People don't believe me. When I say things to them, they think I'm being sarcastic, not sincere. Even when I'm being totally sincere, they think I'm joking."

"And what is the result that you want to have, instead of that?"

"I want people to believe me!"

"Okay," Doctor Irwin continued. "Where in your childhood do you think this problem came from?"

I thought about it a moment and said, "I don't know where this thought came from, but it just popped into my mind, so I'll say it: when my brother and I were little kids, our father would lie to us about stuff, and then when we'd say 'You're lying' he would give us this big, guilty smile and say 'Do I lie?' and we would know he was lying."

As I stood there thinking, I remembered several times in my life where my being an inordinately smiley person had been pointed out to me. At age twelve in summer camp, my nickname was Smiley. And when I was in training to learn how to be on a men's team, my nickname was Cheshire, as in the cat with the shit-eating grin.

I had always known that I smiled a lot, but I never knew that my subconscious direction to smile all the time was causing confusion in my communication. It was making me come across as a liar, or insincere, and not believable.

"Okay," said Doctor Irwin, "Thoughts create beliefs, and beliefs create reality. Right now, your reality is that people don't feel that you're sincere. What do you have to believe in order to make them feel that you're sincere?"

"I have to believe...that I'm sincere?"

"The bad news is that in your subconscious mind, you think you are lying—especially when you go through the physical motions of smiling when you are talking. That action of smiling when you're talking is linked to the belief that what is being said is a lie. That's been burned into your subconscious mind."

I was blown away by the simplicity of it.

"Now the good news is that you can trick your subconscious mind into believing whatever you want it to believe. There is no right or wrong; there's only what the subconscious mind believes. It believes what it believes only because it was programmed to believe that by repetition. How many times did your father say 'Do I lie?'"

"A million," I sighed.

"Right. So that link has been burned into your subconscious mind through a million repetitions. The way to reprogram your subconscious mind is by repeating a new thought, a new set of instructions, a new program that you want to burn in to your brain to override the old programming.

"Scientists have taken pictures of the brain when it is firing off certain thoughts, and they can physically see the connections between the neurons of the brain lighting up. After seven days of repeating a particular sentence aloud, those neural pathways become established in the brain. After 28 days they become permanent. After ninety days they become a superhighway in the brain—a permanent, repeating program in your subconscious mind."

He paused. "So what is it that you want?"

I knew exactly what I wanted. "I want people to believe that I am honest, sincere, and trustworthy."

"Okay, that's your mantra. If you say that mantra five times a day for ninety days, you will create a permanent neural pathway in your subconscious mind that will replay itself, day after day, as part of the 95 percent of your thoughts that get repeated automatically by your subconscious thinking. You will have retrained your brain."

It is just that simple.

Being an overachiever, and wanting to take no chances, I repeated my mantra twenty–five times a day for one hundred days. I advise you to do the same.

ACTION ITEMS:

1) Identify results that you are getting in your life that you no longer wish to tolerate.

    a) _____

    b) _____

    c) _____

2) Decide what results you would like to have show up in your life in place of the unwanted results you've been getting.

    a) _____

    b) _____

    c) _____

3) Write out a mantra for the two most important results you wish to achieve.

    a) _____

    _____

    b) _____

    _____

These will be the first half of your mantra program.

EXTRA POWER: To give your mantras extra power, you are going to modify them in the following ways.

1) **You are going to add emotion to your mantras.** For example, which is more powerful? "I weigh 180 pounds" or "I deserve to weigh 180 lbs"?

2) **You are going to make your mantras time-based.** You're going to be saying these mantras for ninety days, so you're going to add that deadline onto the mantra so that you'll be moving towards a specific goal.

For example, "I deserve to be earning $24,000 or more by February 14, 2010 or sooner, and I am grateful to be a person who can earn $24,000 or more each month."

Deserving and feeling grateful for things are two of the most powerful emotions. I remember a few years ago when I was paying $482 a month to lease a Jeep Grand Cherokee, and one day towards the end of that lease I saw an ad for a BMW X5 for around $539 a month.

I realized that for just a little bit more than I was already paying, I could be driving my dream car. In fact, I pretty much deserved a BMW for what I'd been paying! The very next day I went out and bought that X5.

3) **Your mantras must be believable.** You have to be able to believe that your mantra is possible. If you can't visualize yourself achieving it when you say it, the mantra is not going to work.

If you are currently unemployed and broke, you are most likely not going to become a millionaire in ninety days, and your subconscious mind is just not going to buy it. Likewise, if you weigh three hundred pounds, you're probably not going to shrivel up into Twiggy in ninety days either.

If you want to set longer range goals, anything is possible given enough time, and your subconscious mind will bring together the people and circumstances to create just about any reality—given enough time in a timeline—to make it believable.

For example, the mantra I ended up repeating to myself twenty-five times each day for fifteen months was, "I am honest sincere and trustworthy, and because I am honest sincere and trustworthy I will have ten million dollars in personal assets by 2012."

ACTION ITEMS:

1) Revise your mantras so that they are charged with emotion, time-specific, and believable.

a) _____

_____

b) _____

_____

In order to boost the power of your mantras even more, you are going to create a second half for each of your mantras. This second half will be a visualization mantra that you will also repeat twenty-five times each day, and as you say it each time you will visualize yourself already having achieved the goal of the mantra.

For example, after twenty-five repetitions of the mantra, "I deserve to be earning $24,000 each month as of February 14, 2010, and I am grateful to be a man who can earn $24,000 or more each month," I then said the second half of the mantra twenty-five times: "It is now February 14, 2010 and I am earning at least $24,000 each month. I am proud and excited about my income, I inspire those around me, and I am grateful to be a man who can earn $24,000 each month."

Here is an example of a weight-loss mantra based on something I heard from Doctor Irwin: "I deserve to weigh 180 pounds or less by January 1, 2010 or sooner. I am proud and excited to be trim in my new clothes, I inspire those around me, and I am grateful to be in optimal health."

This would be followed by, "It is now January 1, 2010 and I weigh 180 pounds or less. I am proud and excited to be trim in my new clothes, I inspire those around me, and I'm grateful to be in optimal health."

Now write out both halves of your two complete life-changing mantras:

1)_____

_____

2)_____

_____

If you want help creating a great mantra for yourself, just shoot me an email with 1) What you want to achieve, and 2) What you think the mantra should be. I'll be glad to go over it and improve it for you.

Send your request to Mantras@TheLastYearOfYourLife.com and put the word "mantra" in the subject line. Don't put anything else in the subject line, just the word "mantra." I'm happy to help.

"Emancipate yourself from mental slavery;
none but ourselves can free our mind."
–Bob Marley

"Something for You"

I received a call today from a program participant in Kansas. Let's call her Dorothy.

After the introductory niceties, Dorothy said, "Clint, I'm stuck. I feel like I'm not getting anywhere."

"What do you mean?" I replied.

"I'm working all day long, working harder that you can believe. I'm doing a million things, and at the end of the day I feel like I haven't accomplished anything. I feel empty."

"Tell me, Dorothy, of those million things you do each day, what are you doing for you?"

There was a long silence.

"Dorothy, what are you doing for yourself?"

More silence. Then, "Nothing, I guess."

"That's why you don't feel like you're getting anywhere. You're just running yourself ragged, and not taking anything or any time for you."

This program is about getting the most you can possibly get from The Last Year of Your Life, but none of that will matter if you don't do things for you. Personal things. Things that will make you feel nourished. Things that will make you feel as though you are alive.

I wanted Dorothy to begin with something small and easy, so I asked if she exercised. I was going to suggest walking every day, which is great because it's both physical and meditative.

"Oh, I get plenty of exercise around the farm taking care of the goats and mending fences and everything I do. I get plenty of exercise."

"Okay," I said, "how are you doing with this program? Are you doing all the homework?"

"Oh yes, I'm up to date on all the course material and all the homework. I haven't written my mantras yet, but I believe in them, and I'm going to…"

"Okay, so let's go over your CPR and find something on there that you can do for you," I said, "something you have total control over, so that at the end of each day you can feel like No matter what else, I got THAT for ME. For some people, this program has to start very small, just so you can get a little momentum going for you. Success is all about momentum. Let's find something small you can do for yourself each day so you can feel like you're winning."

The first item she read off her CPR was, "Developed a Daily Spiritual Practice."

"Dorothy, how are you doing with that?"

"I'm not doing anything about that." She sounded very disappointed when she said this.

"Okay," I said, "That's a good result. We'll keep that result in mind. Keep reading."

She read a few results that had to do with projects she wanted to accomplish around the farm, some technical skills she wanted to develop in order to be able to promote her business, and three more that I thought were particularly of interest: "Go on at least one date a week with my husband," "learn to play my harp," and, "learn how to tell fortunes with cards."

It was a very solid CPR overall, and I told her so. It had a great mix of concrete and ethereal results, and if she got half of them she would have a great year. Then I said, "I like the date your husband result, but that's not going to get you feeling like you won every day. What about the harp?"

"I don't think I have time for it really," she said with a sigh. "I'm thinking about cutting that one."

"And what about telling fortunes with cards? Is that a hobby that you have passion about?"
"It's something I'd like to do; I want to learn how..." Her voice trailed off and I didn't sense much commitment there.

"So tell me about the daily spiritual practice. What would that look like? Describe it for me."

"It would start off with meditation, and then it would have yoga practice. Maybe some prayer."

"And if you did that, how much time would it take?"

"Maybe twenty to thirty minutes a day."

It was too easy. The answer to her problem was the number–one result she had listed on her CPR. But she couldn't see it because (a) it was right in front of her face, and (b) it was happening to her, and when you're the one in the hot seat, sometimes it's hard to see the obvious.

"Now imagine how great it would feel if you developed your daily spiritual practice, stuck to it, and made it happen for the rest of the year, every day, getting that yoga practice for yourself. How would that feel?"

"Great!"

"Dorothy, that daily spiritual practice is something you can do! You can have total control over this one part of your day. All you have to do is sit down with yourself and do it...but only you can make it happen."

"Well, how will I start?"

"I think you should just start right when we hang up this phone–call. Take thirty minutes for yourself and go meditate and do yoga and see how that feels. Then tomorrow and the day after that you need to pick a time to do this every day, the same time each day, just for you."

"Like when?"

"Personally," I confided, "if I don't do my daily exercise routine first thing in the morning, more often than not it doesn't get done. Something comes up; the day gets real busy. Could you do it first thing in the morning?"

"I guess so."

"Good. So instead of getting a cup of coffee tomorrow morning, and every morning after that, I want you wake up and meditate and do yoga for thirty minutes, and then you'll be starting off every day with a win. You'll start off every day getting something for you. Then the rest of the day will be gravy—anything else you can accomplish will be a bonus because you'll have already won in your daily spiritual practice."

"That's it? It sounds too simple."

"It's like that saying—you should pay yourself first. This will be taking care of you first. And it will send a very subtle signal that you love yourself more, and that will reinforce everything. Just focus on that for a week or two. No matter what happens, you make sure that you get that morning meditation and yoga. After a week let me know how it's going. And by the way, how's your sleep?"

"That's another thing. I barely get six hours a night with everything going on around the farm."

"Okay, I want you to cross out the harp, and write in Got at least seven hours sleep each night. You have to get your rest. Make that a priority."

A lot of people feel like they need to push themselves to the limit, cutting out sleep and needed rest, rationalizing that they'll be able to catch up later, after they've gotten everything else "done" that they need to do. They don't feel like they have the right to get a full night's sleep.

But I'm here to tell you that you not only have the right, but also the responsibility to get all the rest your body requires. You have to get rest! If you don't, you will soon be running on empty, and feeling empty, and running yourself into the ground. And on top of all that, you now officially have my permission to get a good night's sleep every night! I want you to make it a priority. Just like the man who wrote on his CPR, "I want to eat three meals each day," because he needed to maintain a healthy weight, if you're a person who doesn't get enough sleep then you need to put down "Got seven or more hours sleep each night" on your CPR. Make that a priority.

Getting enough sleep is such an easy and great way to get a win on the scorecard for yourself.

I mean, just think about that for a moment. Doesn't the idea of making a good night's rest every night into a priority in your life sound like a great idea? I'll tell you, it makes me feel all warm and fuzzy!

"Dorothy, this fits in perfectly with where we're at in the program, because the next session is about the power of creating one or two little habits that can change your destiny, and this daily spiritual practice and getting a good night's sleep are exactly the kinds of habits I'm talking about."

Week 7. Create A New Destiny For Your Life

"Two roads diverged in a wood, and I —
I took the one less traveled by,
And that has made all the difference."
–Robert Frost, The Road Not Taken

I'm going to tell you how I lost forty pounds in one year without joining a gym, hiring a trainer, or changing my diet.

I'm not telling you this story to impress you, or to make you feel bad about yourself, or to encourage you to lose weight, or to try and get you to change in any way.

I'm telling you this story to illustrate how making a tiny little change can have a huge impact on a person's life over the course of as little as a year's time, and certainly over the course of a lifetime.

This all began about four years ago, when one of the men on my men's team brought us an idea he called "YouDaMan." It's very simple: adopt one or two tiny habits that will change your life in such a way that you will feel like you are "The Man."

At that point in time I was reaching my peak weight, 236 pounds. (If you will recall, when I was in high school, I wrestled in the 145–pound weight class, so this was truly a pinnacle of fatness in my life.) I was actually getting very bummed out about it, and I had to do something to change.

The big problem was that I had gotten so out of shape that I couldn't even do any real exercise anymore. Heck, I could hardly even bend over to tie my shoes!

But I wanted to change. And as soon as I heard about this YouDaMan project, I sensed that it would work for me.

The key was to keep my commitment simple and easy enough that I would be able to follow through with it every day.

So I committed to doing two tiny things.

1) I would take a thirty-minute walk every day.
2) I would drink four big glasses of water every day.

That's it. Those were the only commitments I made.

It was not easy. In fact, for the first thirty days my legs were <u>killing me</u> every night when I'd lie down to go to bed! I'm talking about serious pains!

After sixty days I decided to increase the duration of my walks to forty-five minutes.

My dog was loving me! We would go on walks every single night, and sometimes during the daytime we would walk around the lake in Silverlake. Occasionally my wife would even come with us.

I really started loving my iPhone then. I would talk to men on the team a lot while I was walking, and when they weren't available I would listen to podcasts that I downloaded from iTunes—shows like The MacWhisperer, The Moth, Bloomberg On The Economy, and my favorite discovery at that time, The Dinner Party Download.

I was also very faithful to my other new habit of drinking four giant glasses of water each day.

About ninety days into the program, I read an article in USA Today about people who lost weight and kept it off for more than three years. The key factor that was identified in the article was that the people who kept the weight off consistently had exercised one hour each day. So I increased my walking regime to one hour.

Bam! That was the magic bullet. On New Year's Day that year I weighed in at 196 pounds, having lost a total of forty pounds in less than one year's time, without joining a gym, hiring a trainer, or switching to a special diet.

Your One Degree Project

If you think about a ship sailing in the Pacific Ocean, and imagine that you changed the heading which that ship was on by just one degree, you can see that by the time that ship crossed the sea it would be many hundreds of miles off its original course. Just by changing the course by one degree!

Now think about your life, and imagine that the years of time ahead of you are the ocean of your life. Consider the impact of drinking more water every day...

Or walking for an hour...

Or flossing your teeth every day...

Or eating an apple a day...

Or meditating for five minutes...

Or going to bed before midnight...

Or taking the stairs instead of using the elevator at work...

Or eating fruit for breakfast instead of pancakes and eggs...

Or limiting your television-watching time...

Or reading a new book each week...

Or taking your micro-greens... (whatever microgreens are!)

Or whatever idea for a new habit turns you on.

The key thing here is that you are adding something to your life that wasn't there before, and that this new habit (or two at most) is something that you can commit to, that you can continue to do day in and day out, and that will be positive for you in some way.

I often think about my grandfather and the walks he would take on the boardwalk almost every night after dinner. If I was there he would always invite me to go with him, and I can't remember a single time I said no. Just a simple walk down to the end of the boardwalk and back, around the time the sun would be setting...such fond memories.

And now, these days, when I am out walking as part of my continuing YouDaMan project, I think of him almost every time I carry on that legacy.

ACTION ITEM:

Pick one or two simple habits that you can adopt in your daily life that will change the course of your destiny. Write it (or them) down and commit to doing it every day by signing and dating below.

1) _____

2) _____

SIGNATURE:_____ DATE: _____

"Sow an act, reap a habit.
Sow a habit, reap a character.
Sow a character, reap a destiny."
–George Dana Boardman

Week 8. It's Time For You To "Grow Up" ... Finally!

"Man is not the creature of circumstances; circumstances are the creatures of men.
We are free agents, and man is more powerful than matter."
–Benjamin Disraeli

Some people would say this should have been the first chapter.

Mark Victor Hansen wrote a whole book about this subject, and while I personally worship MVH, I've met other people who don't think so highly of him.

The bottom line is this: taking personal responsibility for your life is one of the absolute key elements of this program.

I have been as guilty as anyone about blaming other people for shortcomings in my life. I have done it many times, and I catch myself trying to skid by with that kind of lameness all the time. But that doesn't make it right!

Whenever I catch myself trying to look for a way to pin blame for anything on anyone else, I try my best to take a look in the mirror and confront the true responsible party.

I have said previously, and I'll say it again here, that I believe we each create our own reality. We are living the exact life that we want to be living. If we didn't want to be living this life, we'd change it, or make the changes we want to in order to make it into the life we want. Since we're not changing, this must be what we want.

So if this is the life you want, take responsibility for that fact. Take responsibility for your actions. Take responsibility for every single aspect of it.

Most importantly, become aware of the many instances each day when you try to place "blame" for events on someone else in your world, be it your wife, husband, parent, kid, nanny, or whomever. Chances are, they are just a facile scapegoat. And worse yet, they are more than likely a feeble target of bitterness and resentment—all of which is just evil juice corroding your internal organs and your soul.

Now let's get very, very basic with this concept. Imagine you are out on a softball diamond, and you step up to the plate with your bat and get ready to whack a good shot if it comes your way. The first pitch that comes at you is a beautiful lob that drifts right by you in the strike zone, but you don´t swing...and the umpire calls a strike. Zero and one.

The next pitch is another nice one, and you swing, but foul it off to the right side, and now the count is no balls, two strikes.

The third pitch is a good fastball, so you swing for the fences and completely miss.

Three strikes, you're out.

Now, tell me something: who struck out?

Write that person's name on the line:

_____

Okay. So the answer is obvious. But it's not always so easy to see it in every situation in life.

I am amazed at how many times I catch myself trying to place blame for my eff-ups on my wife. In my mind, I immediately try to find a way to make it her fault. And when I do catch myself, I get very mad at myself for being so weak.

So why are we so quick to look for a way out of taking personal responsibility?

Write down some reasons:

Would "looking good" and "saving face" be among them?

Now ask yourself a question: What's more important, looking good or getting the job done?

Let me share a little story of how this all came into focus in my life. I was a struggling and frustrated screenwriter for many years. The way it works in Hollywood is that writers write the scripts, they get an agent who sells the scripts to the producers or studios, and then the agents send the money from the sales to the writers.

The writers don't sully their precious fingers with the crassness of the commerce, so for many years I had an aversion to sales.

Amazingly, I wasn't making very much money. By the end of my screenwriting career I had been driving a taxi on weekends for three years to pay my bills.

I got seriously worried that I was never going to get out of my rut, and I started getting life coaching from my brilliant coach, Paul Roth, whose most powerful piece of advice for me was "I only want you to do projects that you can directly control all aspects of yourself."

Man, what a difference that made in my life!

After ten years of not being responsible for sales or production of my work, I had a huge feeling of impotence. I didn't feel like I could make things happen! Until my experiences in Hollywood, I had ruled the world! (Trust me.) But after ten years of waiting for other people to do things for me, I was addicted to disappointment, and addicted to waiting for other people to do things for me. And the sad truth of the matter is that, so far in my experience of life, nobody wants to do anything for anybody else. (Unless you pay them a lot of money, and they don't even really want to do it then.)

Only when I took Paul's advice, and started restricting my efforts to projects that I had total control over, was I able to get things happening in my career and my life.

This has been a cornerstone of all my work in business since then, and it has stood me well, especially in real estate. While my brother-in-law missed the entire real-estate boom screwing around with partnerships, I never had a partner on a real estate deal, and I was able to get five houses built and four sold.

Another friend of mine bought a fixer-upper house on the East Coast, and because he took on a partner who was a contractor, he missed the peak by four months and ended up losing twenty thousand dollars on the deal after a year and a half of work.

By focusing on projects that I had total control over—that I had clear and full responsibility for—I was able to cut out that habit of waiting for others to do things for me, I was able to get my projects done and complete, and I was able to make a bunch of money.

The bottom line of this week's work is this: unless you are willing to take full responsibility for your life, right now, from here on out and forevermore, you are just kidding yourself; you are not going to accomplish one-tenth of what you are capable of accomplishing; and you are guaranteeing that you are going to be disappointed, let down, and unfulfilled in your life.

The only way you can really feel fulfilled is if you take total responsibility for the things you do. When you do, and when you succeed at what you attempt, only then will you feel like you deserve the accolades. Only when you really do things will you really feel like you accomplished anything.

ACTION ITEM:

Cook yourself a recipe for a meatloaf, or an apple pie, or anything that is a little challenging for you. It should have several steps, several ingredients, and be a recipe that you have never cooked before. It should also be something you want to eat! Go to the grocery store and buy all the best ingredients, checking every apple to make sure it is perfect, or every mushroom to see that it is not dented. Make sure you have the freshest and best of everything, and the best recipe you can find.

Then go home and put it all together with the utmost care and attention to detail. Then sit down with your best dishes and silverware, and savor the flavors and experience of eating that meal which you took total responsibility for.

Write a few sentences about how the food tastes compared to how this same dish has tasted in the past when other people have made it for you.

_____

_____

_____

_____

_____

_____

Now write a few sentences about your reflections on the experience of taking personal responsibility for this meal. How did it feel? How do you feel now about yourself in relation to the food? How do you feel about your ability to get things done and make them happen?

_____

_____

_____

_____

_____

_____

On a scale of 1 to 100, rate your satisfaction with the food: _____

Week 9. Get Healthier
(Lose Weight, Quit Smoking, Get In Shape, etc.)

"The greatest wealth is health."
–Virgil

Think about how lucky we are to be living at this moment in history when it comes to health.

We have the greatest access to medical knowledge and care that has ever been available.

We have organic foods available in almost every supermarket, and farmers markets make accessing the freshest produce easy and fun.

We have a forty-hour workweek that allows us more free time than any civilization has ever had before to focus on our health or any other issue we care to.

We've got gym memberships, fitness trainers, P90X DVD programs, miles of beautiful beaches, boardwalks, and parks to get out and walk in.

We have more time money and opportunity to do anything we want to do for ourselves.

And yet 34 percent of our population is obese, and 60 percent is overweight.

I know that in my own life I have put off getting in shape and making good health a priority at times, and that has been a huge mistake.

If you don't have your health, what do you have?

I remember a few months ago, I was lying in bed in agonizing pain when my legs were killing me, thinking to myself, Please don't let me be crippled! Please let me walk again!

Good health is a gift, but it's a gift that every one of us can go out and do something about.

ACTION ITEMS:

1) Start with the simplest indicator of health: your weight. Type this URL into your web browser and go to the Weight Watchers website to find out your suggested weight range based on height.

http://www.weightwatchers.com/health/asm/calc_healthyweight.aspx

If you are not within your suggested weight range, then make this a result item on your CPR. If you have to lose or gain weight, you want to get into the suggested range. (I have been hugely inspired by a man who wrote on his CPR one year that he wanted to "Eat three meals each day" because he had trouble maintaining weight.)

According to WeightWatchers.com, my weight range is between

_____ and _____ pounds.

Today my actual weight is _____pounds.

This year I need to gain/lose _____pounds to get into the range I should weigh.

2) Evaluate your health according to the questionnaire below.

    a) Five years ago I was <u>healthier</u> / <u>not healthier</u> than I am today.

    b) My main health shortcomings are a result of

            – Less-than-perfect diet/nutrition
            – Not enough exercise
            – Smoking
            – Alcohol/drug abuse
            – Stress

3) According to the National Sleep Foundation, different ages of people have different needs for sleep. The chart below is from their website.

Find your age range on the chart and determine if you are getting as much sleep as you should.

How Much Sleep Do You Really Need?	
Age	**Sleep Needs**
Newborns (1-2 months)	10.5-18 hours
Infants (3-11 months)	9-12 hours during night and 30-minute to two-hour naps, one to four times a day
Toddlers (1-3 years)	12-14 hours
Preschoolers (3-5 years)	11-13 hours
School-aged Children (5-12 years)	10-11 hours
Teens (11-17)	8.5-9.25 hours
Adults	7-9 hours
Older Adults	7-9 hours

Week 10. Experience True Happiness

"Happiness comes from facing challenges and going out on a limb and taking risks.
If you're not willing to take a risk for something you really care about,
you might as well be dead."
–Andrew Schneider

What really makes you happy?

Really happy.

I can hardly think of a better or more important question to ask oneself.

If you have all the money in the world and you're miserable, then all that money is worthless.

I'm reminded of a scene at the end of the movie Up in the Air. George Clooney is sitting in first class with the legendary, top American Airlines pilot who welcomes him into his super-elite status and compliments him on being the youngest ten-million-miler to ever reach that pinnacle of frequent flight, and by that time the achievement means nothing to Clooney's character anymore.

What an elusive target this happiness thing can be.

So how do you isolate what really, truly, honestly, deep down makes you happy? That's what we're going to work on right now.

ACTION ITEMS:

1) What is/was your favorite hobby?_____

2) When you were a little kid, what did you like to do best? _____

_____

3) When you close your eyes and imagine yourself having the best time on vacation, where are you and what are you doing? _____

_____

4) Have you ever lied to your boss (or anyone) so that you could "play hooky" from work or school to do something? What was that thing?

_____

5) What have you always wanted to do "someday" when you have enough time or enough money to do whatever you want?

_____

6) Ask someone who really knows you well what they think is your favorite pastime, occupation, hobby, or personal pursuit. Write down their answer:

_____

7) If you had all the money in the world, all the time in the world, and could do any one thing, what would that one thing be?

_____

8) Imagine you are walking along a deserted beach, and you come across a little silver bottle. You pick up the bottle and rub some of the salt off it. Suddenly it begins to tremble and smoke, and then right in front of you materializes twenty-five-year-old Barbara Eden.

She says, "Master, I can grant you any three wishes."

If a genie granted you three wishes, they would be:

a) _____

b) _____

c) _____

Okay, now that you've spent a good amount of time fantasizing and looking at happiness from all different angles, let me ask you a simple question.

What makes you happy?

_____

_____

_____

_____

_____

Week 11. Really Connect with Family and Friends

"He who throws away a friend is as bad as he who throws away his life."
–Sophocles

Relationships with family and friends provide the richness of life, and yet somehow these are the very same people who get under our skin the most and the easiest.

How is this possible, and how can we do something about it so that we can move forward in life with stronger relationships with the ones we care most about?

Resentment is such a bitter burning force inside of us. It is the great destroyer of family relations, of friendships, of people's lives.

The thing about families is that these relationships with our kin are intense and intimate dynamics that continue over long periods of time. Over the course of time, inevitably come many disappointments, many errors, many injuries, many forgotten birthdays, and the like.

It is this multi-year nature of family life that creates the set of circumstances in which the seeds of resentment can so perfectly be sown. Soon those seeds become giant bushes and even trees, blossoming and filling our inner greenhouse with thriving poisons.

Resentment is a poison—a poison pill that you take with the expectation that it will kill the other person.

How smart is that?

Under what other circumstances would you take poison with the intent of killing someone else?

But you'll do it with the members of your family who have wronged you.

You'll do it with your closest friends who let you down, even if they didn't mean to.

You'll do it with your mother or father who, after all, are merely human beings, trying the best they can to do their best with the set of circumstances they inhabit.

So you end up carrying around this heavy brooding weight on your shoulders day after day—not like a migraine headache, but more like an ingrown toenail, omnipresent, just throbbing annoyingly all the time until you step on it the wrong way and make it zing!

How smart is that?

And what's the net result?

The net result is that you create this giant black hole relationship with your own parent or sibling or ex-whatever, and you spend hours every day trying to not think about the pain, trying to pretend that it doesn't bother you, trying to act like everything in your life is perfect...when it's not.

All it would take would be a phone call.

All it would take would be an ounce of forgiveness, of compassion, of understanding that the other person is a human being, warts and all.

But that's too tough to do with the family and closest friends who have done such horrible things to us.

That's too tough to do for a mother or a father who gave you life.

That's too tough to do for the brother or sister who you shared your childhood with.

That's too tough to do for the person who used to be your best friend.

ACTION ITEMS:

1) Call your mother and/or father (if you're lucky enough to have them still living on this Earth) and tell them that you love them. (Initial in the blank spaces when you have done it.)

MOM: _____
DAD: _____

Tell your mom and dad how much you appreciate the life they've given you.

MOM: _____
DAD: _____

Tell them how great it is to be alive today, and that you couldn't have done it without the gift of life they gave you.
MOM: _____
DAD: _____

2) Call your brother(s) and/or sister(s) and tell them how much you appreciate having them in your life. Just share some old stories with them of a few fond memories you have from your childhood days together.

BROTHER(S) _____
SISTER(S) _____

3) Call up your old best friends that you haven't spoken to in a while and tell them how much their friendship has meant to you over the years. Chew the fat with them for a few minutes.

Friend 1: _____

Friend 2: _____

Friend 3: _____

EXTRA CREDIT: Take pictures of yourself with your family and best friends (shot today, if humanly possible) and paste them onto this page.

Week 12. Appreciate The Fleeting Nature of Life

"Life is too brief. I had a friend whom I intended
to know better. Yesterday he died."
–David Grayson

My Dad passed away in November of 2006.

I talked to him on the phone on a Monday and he sounded fine. He checked himself into the hospital the following Wednesday. On Saturday at 2 p.m. he was a grotesquely puffed–up corpse.

That was it.

I was there in the hospital with him Thursday, Friday, Saturday...there was nothing we could do.

A friend of mine called to see how he was doing on Friday. All I could say was that he was resting comfortably. He was all doped up on morphine waiting for the end to come, and the nurses would check with him and say, "Are you in any pain?"

He'd shake his head no.

It was just a matter of time. And the time passed quickly.

I had been talking to him just about every day for the last three years of his life. Then after he died, I'd want to call him all the time, out of habit as much as anything. But I couldn't call him anymore. He was gone.

That is the fleeting nature of life.

One day you're here. The next day you're gone.

And there's nothing you can do about it, because once you're dead, you are dead. It's over.

*****

My ex-brother-in-law blew his head off last year.

I remember when I got the call. My wife and I were in Caesars Palace; I was visiting clients of my butter business, and we were right in front of Bobby Flay's Mesa Grill when my iPhone rang.

It was my daughter calling. She said, "Daddy!" and that's all she could say because she was hysterically crying.

She handed the phone to my mother, who said, "Brinkley shot himself in the head and killed himself."

In my mind I wanted to call him up immediately and tell him "Don't do it!" But it was already done. Death is final.

Once life is gone it is gone.

That is the fleeting nature of life. It can be here one second and gone the next.

*****

On August 15th my wife and I got home from an amazing and fun weekend trip. We saw Buddy Guy perform an incredible blues concert at Buffalo Bill's

Casino at State Line, Nevada, and my wife even won a thousand dollars playing video poker! We ate, we partied, and we had so much fun.

But when we got home our cat, Opal, was nowhere to be seen.

Opal was the greatest cat in the world. Every single person that met her fell in love with her. She really understood "The Secret Weapon of The Wharton Business School" (as I explain in my book, Free New Power) which is to "assume the rapport." She loved everyone and everyone loved her.

I remember the last time I saw Opal. I was taking a shower, and she jumped up on the counter to reach her paw into the crack of the shower door, trying to touch me. I looked at her and poked at the glass next to her paw for a few seconds, then finished my shower without thinking much else about it.

But it turned out that was the last time I would ever see the greatest cat in the world—the cat I'd bottle-fed from the time she was a little baby. Perhaps my favorite pet ever.

In retrospect she seemed to have a look on her face like, Don't you know I'm going to be gone when you get back?

I didn't know. She was only six years old, and I thought we'd have her love in our lives for at least another decade!

But when we got back on that Sunday she was gone, never to be heard from or seen again.

That's the fleeting nature of life.

Here one moment, gone the next.

*****

I was talking about all this stuff with a friend of mine who's a cop.

He goes, "That's nothing. I rolled up on a call the other night, and this woman went out to the liquor store, a car came out of nowhere and crashed into her through a plate-glass window. She's dead. Her family thinks she just went to the liquor store and she'll be home any minute. They're waiting for her to get home, but she's gone!"

This stuff happens.

You never know when your number will be up.

"That's why I never leave the house without telling my wife I love her," said my cop friend. "No matter if we're fighting, no matter what. I'll say, this argument isn't over, we're not done fighting, but I gotta go, so I love you and I'll see you later."

ACTION ITEMS:

1) Write the names of three people or pets that you have known in your life and jot down a sentence or two about how they disappeared from your life forever.

   a) _____ – _____

   _____

   b) _____ – _____

   _____

   c) _____ – _____

   _____

2) Watch the movie Saving Private Ryan.

3) Watch the movie Time After Time starring Christopher Reeve.

4) Go to one of these websites and spend thirty to forty-five minutes reading about how famous people have died:

   www.thedeadrockstarsclub.com

   www.howtheydied.net

   www.cinemorgue.com

Week 13. Develop a Personal Vision for Your Life

By Jessica C. Bollinger, LCSW, MSW www.imagoconnection.com

"Stop thinking in terms of limitations
and start thinking in terms of possibilities."
– Terry Josephson

This past Sunday at our Unitarian church, I was asked to speak about my own personal vision. Our church community is working on a vision for the church. Our minister thought it would be helpful if the congregation could get a sense of what visions can mean to us on a personal level.

My vision is small: "Healing the world one couple at a time." How did that vision begin? I can remember sitting in my masters of social work class and the professor looked out at us and asked, "How many of you chose getting your masters because of a difficult event that happened to you in your life?"

I raised my hand. I looked around and everyone else had his or her hands raised.

We are who we are by our experiences. We make our choices because of our experiences.

Having a "vision" helps you put the road in place to have the experience that you want.

Why did I go back to school to get masters of social work? I had just had the heart-wrenching experience of a relationship ending, and my partner who was the biological mother took our child. Ben was three and a half. I was the primary caregiver. He was my life.

Many times, our visions are based on something bad that happens to us, and we want to change things so that it doesn't happen to others.

After this happened with Ben, I thought to myself, "I don't ever want this to happen to children—where they get 'caught' between their caregivers' relationship and hurt by separation".

This had happened to me when I was a child. My parents divorced when I was about twelve. No matter how easy my parents tried to make it on us, we knew that it was difficult for them. That was thirty-nine years ago. As kids my sister and I adapted to what we needed to do to help the situation.

When that happened with Ben, I made a conscious decision: "I am going to help couples so that this never happens where children are put into the middle."

A vision is like a rudder on a boat—it ends up unconsciously steering us to where we really need to go to succeed at that vision.

My Dad always had a boat on the Ohio River as I was growing up. I like to use that metaphor. I can remember being a little kid at the helm, feeling big, feeling close to my Dad, sitting up on the pilots seat with a cushion underneath me so I could see better. He would tell me to "Look up ahead at that mile-marker on the shoreline, and steer for that".

I would keep the boat in that direction, adjusting for speed and current, moving out of the way of barges and other craft. As I would get closer to the mile-marker on the shoreline, I would readjust to a new point to steer towards.

When I would look back over the rear of the boat, I could see my path in the water. It was not a straight line. The currents had carried it; the adjustments for other vessels had made it curve a bit. But I could see where I had come from, and it was pretty direct.

My vision of helping couples took me on the path I was supposed to be on.

We know we are on the right vision if:

Things feel "right."

We feel comfortable in our body with this vision.

Serendipitous things happen along the way to help us along on this vision.

We feel positive, with a positive purpose.

So here I was, an MSW graduate. I was working at Catholic Social Services as a counselor.

And then a big barge appeared in my path. My new relationship was in trouble; I felt like a hypocrite trying to help couples when mine was in trouble.

I happened upon an article in the **Family Therapy Networker Magazine** titled, "A New Way to Love." It was an article about Imago Relationship Therapy and how it gives tools to have a great relationship.

I looked it up online and I found a workshop—the "Getting the Love You Want" workshop. We attended. It was down in the Maggie Valley in North Carolina.

It was very life-changing, and gave us the tools to have a conscious, intentional relationship.

I became trained and certified. It changed my practice.

Relationships are the "test." We cannot NOT be in relationship. We are always in relationship—with our boss, our coworkers, our kids, our families, our partners.

Visions are conscious and intentional. They are our spiritual practice.

Staring at the mile marker ahead.

If couple-hood is loving and respectful, where two whole, fully alive selves can be fully differentiated—where the two can cross the bridge into the other's world and it can make sense to them—they don't have to agree or disagree. They can be a witness to each other.

This creates a relationship environment where children can truly prosper—where the parents can truly live consciously and intentionally and meet the needs of their children.

And then the children grow up to live consciously. They grow up with no baggage of unmet needs. They have a model of how to have a good relationship from their caregivers. They witness wonderful communication; they feel the environment of respect and love.

Thus it is healing the world, one couple at a time.

It is a vision. The vision gives me a path. The path winds and curves, but keeps me on course. It gives me hope and satisfaction.

And this conscious form of communication, called the "intentional dialogue" that Imago teaches—being able to cross the bridge into the other's world—has been presented at the United Nations.

At conferences I have witnessed an Israeli and a Palestinian practice this dialogue. Crossing the bridge into each other's worlds, they see that they both want the same thing—their children to be safe.

So in summation:

> A vision is formed out of our past experiences.

> It is a roadmap that helps us stay on course.

> It creates the occurrences and things along the path that support that vision.

> The vision is correct for us if our body feels good with it.

> Our visions give us hope and purpose.

> Our visions are good for other people and the world.

> Visions help us live intentionally and consciously. They are part of who we are—our core—thus a vision is our spiritual practice.

> The vision attracts what we need to learn to keep moving towards that vision.

ACTION ITEMS:

1) What is the defining event of your life that has shaped your personal vision?

_____.

2) What events have occurred along your life-path to support your vision?

A) _____

B) _____

C) _____

3) How is your vision for your life good for other people and the world?

_____

_____

4) What things have you learned because they have been attracted to you so that you could keep moving towards your vision for your life?

_____

_____

Week 14. Learn How To Instantly Turbo-Charge Your Personal Power (Like The Movie Stars Do It)

"The secret of health for both mind and body
is not to mourn for the past,
nor to worry about the future,
but to live the present moment wisely and earnestly."
–Buddha

Why are we so fascinated by movie stars?

And why do they get paid millions of dollars to do their "jobs"?

The answer is surprisingly simple: movie stars are living each moment more fully present than the rest of us mere mortals, and that's why they look like they are living a more intense version of reality than everyone else. They are riveting to watch because they are quite literally "more alive" than regular people are.

How do they do that? And how can any of us do that? Thankfully, these answers, too, are surprisingly simple.

When I was in my late twenties, I came to the sudden realization that I wanted to be a movie star, and that this had truly been my lifelong dream. So I enrolled in the Howard Fine Acting Studio and started studying acting at what was then the top acting school in Hollywood, with Howard Fine himself —the man who was considered The Primo Guy.

One of the very first and simplest things we learned at the Howard Fine Acting Studio was the technique of using our senses to become instantly more present in the moment. "Look, listen, touch, taste, smell what is going on around you," Howard explained. "This will instantly connect you to the experience you are having in the moment."

You see, being present in the moment is what "good acting" is all about. When you watch the great ones on the silver screen, it doesn't look like they are remembering lines, or sleepwalking through their lives up there. It looks like they are experiencing things for the first time, freshly—discovering every thought, emotion, and idea.

That's what you want to do.

You want to be present to the experience of your senses in each and every moment, as opposed to living unconsciously...as opposed to sleepwalking or daydreaming your way through life...as opposed to numbing yourself out with drugs, alcohol, or plain old laziness.

If you want to live each day more fully present in the moment, do what the movie stars do: look, listen, touch, taste, and smell what's going on around you.

ACTION ITEM:

When you catch yourself "zoning out" or daydreaming this week, force yourself to be present in the moment by using your senses to live more actively. Do this at least five times this week, and make notes about your experiences in the white space and margins of this page.

Week 15. Trust Yourself Completely

"A man who doesn't trust himself can never truly trust anyone else."
–Cardinal de Retz

There comes a point in your life where you begin to understand that you have an intuitive power inside your gut—a power that knows.

In your gut you know when you are doing something stupid.

You know when you are about to make a move that is wrong.

Yet you do it anyway...

And cringe.

ACTION ITEM:

Write down a time when you knew something was hugely wrong and yet you did it anyway: _____.

What was the cost when you went against your gut feeling or instincts that time?

_____

_____

_____

_____

_____

It's as though there's an alarm system inside each of us, and when you are about to make a lame move, the buzzers start to sound. It's just amazing.

Contrast that to when you do things that are right, that are good for you—how easy it feels, and what little resistance there is.

I remember when I met my wife. Nothing could have been easier; there was no resistance; everything just clicked.

And when I made up my mind to go to Wharton, it made perfect sense to me from the very first moment—that was exactly what I was going to do. And every single step forward towards that goal clicked naturally into place.

ACTION ITEM:

Write down some of the smart decisions you've made, and some of your thoughts on how easy those decisions were to make.

a)

b)

c)

You know when you are doing the right thing, and when you're doing the wrong thing. The key is to trust yourself.

Week 16. Deepen Your Character

"The saddest failures in life are those that come from
not putting forth the power and will to succeed."
–Edwin Percy Whipple

Whenever we send men off to do initiation events, I try to remember to leave them with my general perspective on self-development work: there's always more you can get; there's always something else to discover; you can always go deeper.

The last big event I attended was for graduates only, meaning that every man at the event had already graduated from the Men's Weekend. That was intense. We got right into it, and stayed deep the whole time.

So I really challenged myself to go as deep as I could go.

I had a headache from screaming. I lost my voice on the first day and could barely speak for a week.

At one point I feared that I might be having a heart attack...but I kept going.

And am I ever glad I did.

Where I got to was the most profound and deepest emotional experience of my entire life. I had no idea that I could get so deep. I had no idea that I could be so sad. I had no idea that I could be so human. I had no idea that my soul was so profound.

That was the day that I discovered true compassion within me.

That was the day when I discovered true courage within me.

That was the day that I discovered who I truly was as a man.

ACTION ITEM:

From this day forward, until the very last moment of The Last Year of Your Life, I want you to go deeper.

Every single time that you think you've given it your all—that you've gone as deep as you can get—I want you to dig deeper and call upon unknown reserves of personal power and fortitude.

I want you to push yourself harder than you've ever pushed; I want you to challenge yourself without fear of consequences; and I want you to keep going and going and going until you are exhausted.

Will you do that?

"I promise to push myself harder every time. I promise to challenge and surpass my expectations every time. I promise to go deeper every time."

_____   _____

signature   date

Week 17. Access A Super-Power That You Are Suppressing

"Anger is a great force. If you control it, it can be transmuted
into a power which can move the whole world."
William Shenstone (1743–1763)

Getting in touch with your anger may not be the epitome of being "PC" (or politically correct). It's not polite to be angry. It's not attractive. It's not the way to win friends and influence people.

But anger is real. It is living inside of you. It is growing every single day that the pressure is not relieved. It is eating you up. It is burning you up. It's festering in your guts, in your heart, and in your soul.

And if you don't do something about it, that anger will ruin your life, or kill you, or both.

So that's why we're going to go after it right now, this week, while there are still thirty-six weeks left in The Last Year of Your Life.

ACTION ITEMS:

Find a safe, quiet, well-insulated place to do this work. A basement is perfect. If you can't have the house all to yourself, warn the other occupants that there could be some loud screaming or noise because you are working on a self-help project.

1) Listen to this song: "I Hate You" by Slayer
http://www.youtube.com/watch?v=TAXzGkzj5E8

2) List the three people who have screwed you over the worst in your life, or cheated you, or thrashed your heart the harshest, or ignored you, or belittled you, or made you feel worthless—the worst people who have crapped on you most painfully in your whole life.

a) _____

b) _____

c) _____

3) What did those people do to you?

a) _____

_____

b) _____

_____

c) _____

_____

Try to feel the burn that these people put on you. Play that song while you look at pictures of those people, and try to let the anger and hatred that you feel towards them bubble up. Don't fight it. Surrender to it.

Allow yourself to release any words of pain and hatred that come up from the depths.

Give yourself permission to not make sense, to say anything that you want to or feel like saying, regardless of what it sounds like or means.

Take a ride on the Hatred Express and just go with it.

This may not feel good. This probably won't be fun. This definitely will make your blood boil, and it could give you a headache.

Shout it out...

Scream it as loud as you can...

Don't edit yourself...

Let go...

Trust the process.

If you want to watch a demonstration of this exercise, go to http://www.thelastyearofyourlife.com/The_Last_Year_Of_Your_Life/Anger.html

But keep in mind that your personal anger session need not resemble the demonstration video. It should be loud; it should come from deep within you; it should make your face red; but other than that, it's all your own experience.

Keep going until you are done. It's your own personal process, so just be okay with whatever happens.

Good luck!

More on Anger

You may find that you uncover feelings of anger that you did not know were present inside you. That's good. That's the point.

Anger is a natural and super-powerful emotion that has a mind of its own and will run its course, somehow, through your body.

It is an emotional energy force, and unless you allow it to exit your body through emotional release, it will find a way to get out through some physical escape route, manifesting itself as bleeding ulcers, headaches, constipation, diarrhea, heart disease, skin problems, and even cancer.

The much better and easier way to let it out is through our anger exercise.

If you do this work "correctly" you will probably experience hoarseness, a sore throat, or temporary loss of your voice from screaming. You may even get a headache from screaming so much. Every time I do it I've lost my voice, and I have gotten headaches from screaming. But I always push myself to go as far as I can and to give my all to this work, because it is truly powerful.

The first time I did this work was in 2000, and believe me when I tell you I really thought I got all that anger out. I totally went for it! My voice was shot for three days. But when I re-visited this work in 2007, much to my surprise, a lot of the same anger at the same people came up for me, and even more intensely than the first time. Seven years later the full impact of "the wrongs they had perpetrated upon me" were clearer to me in retrospect; the true price that I had paid had been fully revealed through the perfecting lens of time.

Recently a member of the program finished this exercise and called me up, crying. "I'm scared," she said. "I didn't know all this was inside of me. I've worked really hard to avoid these feelings."

I explained to her, "You've tried to pretend all these feelings didn't exist because your ego was trying to protect you from acknowledging the pain, and to keep you looking good to yourself. If you didn't get hurt, you wouldn't look as bad to yourself. But you did get hurt. And now you're getting that emotion up and out so it doesn't fester inside you and come out as cancer or some other physical manifestation."

"I never got mad at that person for screwing me over the way he did," she sobbed. "I tried to focus on other things."

"Doesn't that sound like denial to you? If the person screwed you over, it's only natural to get angry. Angry at them…and at yourself."

She cried and said, "I'm afraid. I don't know what's on the other side."

"On the other side is the authentic you. The real you. The you that doesn't look so perfect. The you with scars and bruises. That's the you that you will finally be getting to know."

Until you know the real you, you are just faking it.

Until you know the real you, and experience what it feels like to be that person, you are living a lie; you're just an actor, not an authentic human being. You're just the Madison Avenue version of who you really are.

I might understand why a person could want to put forth the Madison Avenue version of themselves to employers, or even for new people that they are meeting out in the big bad world, but why would you want to limit your own experience of yourself to a fantasy?

Real human beings have scars.

Real human beings are not perfect.

They've been hurt emotionally, physically, and psychically.

Their egos have been stepped on and ground down into the dust by mean, horrible people, or by people who were not conscious of their actions, or by people who just plain didn't care enough to give a damn.

Those wounds hurt. But those wounds are okay. They are part of living on this Earth. They are real parts of your true and unique life experience.

The key is not to pretend that they don't exist. You have to recognize that the pain is there, lodged deep inside your body and your soul. And once you access that anger, to let it out.

Get it out.

Get it all out.

Week 18. Walk Through "The Portal To Unlimited Power"

"He that wrestles with us strengthens our nerves and
sharpens our skill. Our antagonist is our helper."
–Edmund Burke

I was flipping through an Oprah magazine when I came across a short piece on forgiveness by playwright and actor Tyler Perry.

Here's the part that I felt a strong connection to:

My father was a carpenter. He used his hands to pour concrete and hammer nails. He also used his hands to beat me.

I was a tall child, but sickly—I had asthma—and when I went to work with my father, the sawdust made me cough. I preferred staying home, writing and drawing. I conjured up other worlds: worlds in which I didn't worry about being poor, in which I was someone else's child—a child who lived in a mansion and had a dog.

My father—a man with a third-grade education who was orphaned at two and sent to work in the fields at five—understood only the physical. He thought he could beat the softness out of me and make me hard like him.

When I was twenty-one, I left my house in New Orleans and headed to Atlanta to be a playwright. I got a day job as a bill collector and scrimped and saved to put on my play I Know I've Been Changed— a musical about recovering from an abusive childhood. But even though I was writing about recovering, I wasn't doing it. Every day I felt angry and bitter and terribly lonely. I rarely dated, and if a woman told me she loved me, I headed for the door.

My play bombed; thirty people came on opening weekend. I put it on the next year and the year after that, and each time, it bombed again. Finally, twenty-eight years old, out of money and months behind on rent, I started sleeping in my car.

When the car broke down, I asked my father to cosign on a new one, as he had just done for my sister (the light-skinned daughter he adored). When he refused, I forged his signature. And when the car got repossessed, he called me, yelling. As I sat in that little room I'd just scraped together enough money to rent, listening to him berate me, something snapped. Something dormant in me woke up, and I began to yell back.

I told him that he'd hated me since I was born—that I didn't deserve the things he'd done to me. Everything I'd ever felt or thought—even things I hadn't been aware of—came out. When I was done, the line was silent for a long time. And then, for the first time ever, my father said, "I love you."

After we hung up, I felt light, empty, and exhausted. I knew that I would never again look at my father in hurt or anger. But in a strange way, I also sensed that something had died. I sat crying for hours, as if I were in mourning. My energy source, my fight, my rage that had moved me every day—it was all gone.

Slowly but surely, I began to fuel my days with joy instead of fury. That year —call it coincidence, call it karma—my play sold out. Then it sold out again, and then again.

I began to write new plays, and the theme of forgiveness runs through them all. It's simple: when you haven't forgiven those who've hurt you, you turn your back against your future. When you do forgive, you start walking forward.

I can't get over how powerful this last statement is:

When you haven't forgiven those who've hurt you, you turn your back against your future. When you do forgive, you start walking forward.

Hatred, bitterness, resentment, anger—these are all poisons we generate inside and against ourselves, and these poisons are very busy eating away at our own soul, as surely as acid will eat away a piece of metal.

ACTION ITEMS:

1) Watch this video: How Do I Forgive Someone Who's Hurt Me?
http://www.youtube.com/watch?v=rzbj8BdfW-0

2) Consider how you are feeling the next time you catch yourself muttering resentful thoughts about someone who has done you wrong. Are you feeling happy, exalted, or energized with positive emotion? Or are you feeling tiny, petty, angry, and disempowered?

Write down some notes about how you feel: _____

_____

Think about the power that the person who wronged you has over you and your life. Consider how much time you spend thinking about them and the horribleness they've inflicted upon you—how much time you spend thinking about how much you hate them, and what you'd like to have happen to them as payback.

Do you think that any of the time and energy you are spending on these negative emotions and thoughts actually affects your enemy?

Do you think it affects you?

A study published in Harvard Women's Health Watch states that researchers have discovered that holding a grudge places the same strains on a body as tense muscles, elevated blood pressure, and increased sweating can have.

The same study also presents scientific evidence that forgiveness has health benefits. The researchers found that forgiving people actually reduces stress, improves your heart rate, and helps you to have better blood pressure.

So, apart from the obvious and long-known spiritual benefits of forgiveness, there are awesome physical benefits as well. Reducing your stress levels will allow you to live a healthier, happier life. Taking back control from the person who hurt you gives you the power to take control of and reduce factors that could have detrimental health and psychological impact on your well-being.

Stress has both short- and long-term consequences.

Short-term consequences of stress:

> • Physical symptoms, such as rapid tiredness, headaches, digestive problems, and muscle tension.

> • Emotional and behavioral symptoms, such as disturbed sleep patterns, low self-esteem, mood swings, anxiety, and poor concentration.

Long-term effects of stress can take a toll on one's health, increasing the risk of serious physical and mental problems, including:

- Heart attack or angina
- Increased risk of stroke
- High blood pressure (hypertension)
- Tendency towards depression and other mental health problems

What is Forgiveness, and How Do You Truly Forgive?

I don't believe that forgiveness means turning the other cheek, running away, condoning what the other person has done to you, or giving that person a chance to hurt you again. When you forgive, you're not going to forget about what happened to you, and it doesn't mean you're opening yourself up to it happening to you again.

The American Heritage College Dictionary defines "forgive" as "to renounce anger or resentment against." It comes from a Greek root word meaning "to set free," as in freeing a slave. Poetically, in the act of forgiving, the slave who is set free is your very own self. By forgiving, we emancipate ourselves from slavery to hatred.

And yes, slavery is exactly what it is. Hatred works you, bestowing no positive reward, and it keeps working you until it's done with you. You lose your own willpower in the face of hatred, and you find yourself muttering and thinking hateful thoughts on a subconscious, automatic level throughout your day and during your sleep.

According to the dictionary definition, to forgive is to renounce resentment or anger. It doesn't say anything about forgetting, ignoring, approving of what happened to you, or anything other than just renouncing your anger or resentment.

I know that even the simple act of renouncing your anger or resentment could seem like an impossible task. How can you forgive a murderer, or someone who abused you as a child, or any other heinous criminal act that has been perpetrated against you? How can you surgically cut those feelings out of your heart and soul? And what does that word "renounce" really mean?

American Heritage College Dictionary defines "renounce" as "to reject, disown."

You don't actually have to stop feeling anger or resentment. You just have to renounce anger and resentment, which means disown your anger and disown your resentment.

This is a key distinction. A giant reason why more people don't try to forgive is because they think they can't possibly stop feeling angry, hurt, or vengeful. I'm not telling you to stop feeling any of those things. I'm just telling you not to let those feelings own you. Make an intellectual choice to rise above them.

Whereas feelings of vengeance allow hatred to rule you, the act of forgiveness conquers feelings of hatred, vengeance, and retribution.

But you have to have mental toughness and courage, because it requires a much bigger person to be able to forgive than it does to seek revenge.

Killers, hoodlums, and murderers are the kind of people who seek revenge. Are you a killer, a hoodlum, or a murderer? Is that what you want to become?

If not, then the alternative action which is required is to forgive.

To forgive, all you have to do is decide to give up any urges you have to be angry or resentful. Disown those feelings. Walk away from them. Set yourself free from them!

I know it's not easy. It takes huge amounts of inner strength and courage. But like working out your muscles in a gym, the more inner strength and courage you call upon and use, the more you will have moving forward. So once you begin to forgive a certain person for a certain transgression against you, it will get easier and easier as you get better and better at it.

Remember, I'm not telling you to try to ignore your natural feelings of anger or resentment, or to try to pretend you're not feeling those emotions anymore. I'm just advising you to rise above their enslaving power. You are going to choose to no longer be the slave of anger. I'm asking you to choose to no longer let those "anger tapes" run you like a robot. You and your beautiful self will choose to transcend above those denigrating emotions and dwell instead upon more worthy emotions.

As a human being, you have the power to make that choice for yourself by using your conscious mind. It's amazing and difficult to be able to do it sometimes, but you have that choice. You can set yourself free from those feelings. You can use your willpower to prevent those feelings from owning you—that's what it means to disown them.

When you feel that old slave-driver Hatred starting to whip you into old patterns of submission, you just stand up straight and proud and say your mantra: "I am free from anger and hatred. Instead, I choose to love myself."

This is the true essence of what forgiveness is about: loving yourself. It's about choosing to feel love for yourself instead of hate for the other person. Because all you're really doing when you feel hatred towards another person is filling your own body with the horrible emotional feelings of hatred.

When you're enthralled with feelings of hatred towards someone who wronged you, that other person probably doesn't even know you're alive. But your body is filled with sickening horrible feelings of hatred. Those feelings of hatred poison you, and they poison the way you interact with the whole world.

Set yourself free from those terrible feelings. Choose love instead.

So how do you actually forgive?

1) You choose not to act on the feelings of hatred and vengeance by muttering insults to yourself or shouting them at the other person. You decide to focus your attention elsewhere, just the same way that you could simply choose not to gossip.

For example, imagine you are speeding along the freeway and you come around a corner at eighty-five miles an hour only to see a big, ugly state trooper squad car parked on the side of the road, and a radar gun tracking you.

When the state cop pulls you over, you're probably feeling hatred towards him. But a normal, sane citizen would most likely try to remain calm and polite with the officer because they know that any other behavior would be stupid.

Thanks to our superior intellect, we can make the choice not to act on feelings of anger, just the same way we have control over other natural functions, such as our bladders.

Forgiving means you feel the anger or resentment, and you triumph over it. And when those feelings of anger and resentment come back, you need to shut them down as quickly as possible instead of fanning the flames, because you know that if you do fan the flames, it will be your house burning down, not your enemy's.

2) Try to imagine what horrors might have transformed an innocent little baby into the horrible monster that is your enemy. If you can possibly find some way to empathize with the horrors that your enemy must have gone through in order to become so horrible themselves, then maybe you can start to feel sorry for them—to feel sorry for how twisted and ugly it must be for them to be living with themselves.

If you can do that, you can begin to put yourself in the other person's position, and once you can empathize with them, you can start to love them just a little for being a person who was wounded like you were. And if you can love them just a little, think how huge a person that will mean you have become.

I know this is hard, and maybe even impossible to imagine doing.

But you can try.

At the very least, your hatred will subside.

REMEMBER: Forgiveness is not something we do for other people. We do it for ourselves—so we can get well and move on with our lives.

If you can forgive the people who have hurt you the most, who have been unforgivably cruel and mean to you, then what is beyond your ability? What can't you do? This is the portal to unlimited power. By doing the impossible you create a super-power within you.

"Forgiveness is the sweetest revenge."
–Isaac Friedman

Week 19. This Tiny Decision Will Eliminate Tons of Wasted Time

"You may be deceived if you trust too much,
but you will live in torment if you do not trust enough."
–Frank Crane

Here is the question I want you to ask yourself: how does it feel to not trust a person?

You know how that goes; you're at the airport, you give the skycap your bags, and something about that person makes you feel like he's purposely going to delay your bags and they're not going to make it onto your flight.

How does that feel?

It sucks, doesn't it? Those kinds of feelings make you feel small, weak, and vulnerable—not at all the kinds of emotions you want to be basking and luxuriating in during The Last Year of Your Life.

*****

Among the men's divisions, we have a saying: "Trust is not earned. It's given."

What this really means is that trusting another person is completely an intellectual decision. There may be intuition involved. There may be a period of evaluation. But ultimately it comes down to a simple decision on your part: am I willing to trust this person or not? You can delay bestowing trust on a person until they pass some sort of test or exhibit some kind of trustworthy quality or qualities, but ultimately you must make a decision to either trust or not trust a person.

I didn't go to a dentist from the age of twenty-one until I turned forty-two. No joke. It got to the point that I became afraid to go—afraid to find out what kind of damage had been wreaked upon my chompers.

One day my wife went to a local dentist and suggested that I try him. I did.

Twenty-one years between dental visits, and all I needed was a thorough deep cleaning and one tiny filling. Am I lucky, or what?

The guy did the deep cleaning and the filling and I had no problems with any of it. Perfect!

I went back the next summer for my (now) annual trip to the dentist on my birthday. Same deal: a deep cleaning and one small filling. But this time, the filling did not turn out perfect. In fact, as I'm writing this six months later, it still bothers me. It's sensitive to heat and cold, and it always feels like I have food stuck between that tooth and the one behind it.

I have to find a new dentist; I have revoked my trust of this guy. He's already earned my trust with the perfect work he did the first time. He obviously has the knowledge and skill to do a perfect job, but despite the fact that he's qualified, I am no longer willing to give him my trust.

This is clear proof that trust is given, not earned.

*****

There is an amazing book called The Speed of Trust, and I'm going to borrow one of that book's key concepts and abbreviate it here for you. When trust goes up, speed goes up and cost goes down. Likewise, if trust goes down, speed goes down and cost goes up.

The fantastic example from the book is that since 9/11, we have less trust for everyone participating in commercial airline travel. As a result of trust going down, now you have to get to the airport at least an hour before your flight (speed is down), and you have to pay TSA security fees (cost has gone up) every time you travel. Trust is down; speed is down; cost is up.

*****

ACTION ITEM:

During The Last Year of Your Life, you don't have any time to waste. When trust goes up, speed goes up. Trust is given.

For the rest of The Last Year of Your Life, you are going to trust. Everyone. Everything. Every time. Everywhere. Trust, trust, trust.

Trust me. Trust your buddy. Trust your family. Trust your friends. Trust your coworkers. Trust your customers. Trust your vendors. Trust the waitress and the chef. Trust the gas station attendant. Trust the taxi driver, the hot-dog vendor, the guy at the dry cleaners.

Trust everyone and everything.

Are you going to get burned by this? Maybe, sometimes. But on the whole, you are going to save a lot of time and money.

Write about at least three events this week where you gave someone trust as part of this exercise, and what happened with regard to speed and cost. And how did you feel about being trustful?

1)

2)

3)

Week 20. Feel The Joy Of Truly Loving Other People

"There are four questions of value in life. What is sacred?
Of what is the spirit made? What is worth living for, and what is worth dying for?
The answer to each is the same. Only love."
–Don Juan deMarco (1995)

Some love is easy and automatic, such as the love of a parent for a baby. That's not the love we're going to talk about here.

In The Last Year of Your Life we tackle the hard stuff.

The love that's not always so easy is the love of another person who is above the age of five.

When people stop being helpless, when they start taking actions, when they begin to have an impact on your world and on your life, that's when it can become more difficult to love them.

What makes love so scary and difficult sometimes is that it has such power over you.

When you love a person, you will automatically take their phone calls. You will spend money on them, or give them money, or steal for them, or do anything to help them.

Love is the most powerful emotion on the planet, because it is directly linked to a chemical reaction in the body that creates a sense of safety, well-being, and pleasure.

Adrenaline, dopamine, and serotonin mix as a love cocktail in your bloodstream to alter your sense of reality.

It can make you crazy. Love can literally drive you out of your mind. It can make you self-destruct. It can undermine your personal power and your instincts for self-preservation.

Love can make you do all the wrong things, and yet we want it more than anything.

That's where love's power comes from: our desire and need to have love.

We learn this behavior as a baby. The only way a baby knows it is protected and safe and going to be fed is when it feels love.

Years of this conditioning ingrains this need for love into our subconscious thought patterns—especially the love of a parent. This is why we will grow up and "marry our mother or father."

The love cocktails in our bloodstream take us back to the feeling of safety and well-being we learned as babies.

Being a baby was a great time for most people. All your needs are met, you get tons of attention and affection, and all you have to do is eat and sleep. What could be better?

ACTION ITEMS:

1) Who was the first person you ever loved, and why? _____

_____

_____

2) Who was your first romantic love partner, and what was it about that person that drew you to them? _____

_____

3) Are you in a love relationship now, and is that relationship serving you or hurting you? _____

_____

_____

_____

4) In the best of all worlds, how would you behave in a love relationship?

_____

_____

_____

5) How are you showing up in your current love relationship?

_____

_____

_____

_____

_____

EXTRA CREDIT: Take a great picture of yourself with your lover today and paste it in here. If you're not in a relationship, paste in some pictures of the type of person you would like to be in relationship with.

Week 21. Experience Genuine Compassion for Yourself and Others

"There are three things that are important in human life.
The first is to be kind. The second is to be kind. The third is to be kind."
– Henry James

Nobody has any responsibility to be compassionate towards you, including yourself. You can be the biggest bastard in the world towards yourself if you want to be, and nobody can stop you.

You can beat yourself up all day and night. You can self-criticize. You can self-deprecate. You can eat crappy food.

You can put yourself in positions and life circumstances that don't fulfill you, that endanger your life and limb, that physically do damage to you, and that are emotionally cruel.

We've all done it.

ACTION ITEMS:

Write down three times when you have been mean to yourself.

Physically: _____ _____ _____

Intellectually: _____ _____ _____

Emotionally: _____ _____ _____

Or you could do the opposite! You could be kind to yourself.

You could treat yourself like a person you love. You could be gentle towards your psyche. You could nurture your wounded soul. You could refrain from beating yourself up.

You could take an opportunity, every now and then, to do something that you would really enjoy doing. You could avoid stuff that's unpleasant.

You could give yourself a freaking break!

You could!

ACTION ITEMS:

Write down just one time when you were kind to yourself.

Physically: _____

Intellectually: _____

Emotionally: _____

Now compare how it felt to be mean to yourself those three times to how it felt to be good to you.

Which is more fun? Which feels better? Which is better for you?

The choice is yours.

Every time.

It's easy to see that it's a genuine choice, isn't it?

EXERCISE:

This week I want you to actively make the choice to be kind to yourself, to be nice, to exhibit genuine compassion for yourself at least one time each day. Make notes about each time.

DAY 1:

DAY 2:

DAY 3:

DAY 4:

DAY 5:

DAY 6:

DAY 7:

Many people have an easier time being compassionate towards other people. For one thing, it's not so personal.

Plus, there's less at stake. You're nice, and then they're gone, and you can just forget all about it.

On the other hand, if you have a tough time with it, try to give people the benefit of the doubt; have a little faith that they are doing the best they can in their circumstances.

Nobody starts out in life dreaming of becoming a beggar or a hobo or homeless when they grow up.

At some point everybody had a fantasy that they would become a rock star, or an astronaut, or a rich person driving in a Mercedes with a gorgeous spouse in the hand-stitched, butter-leather bucket seat next to them.

Try to connect with that common thread of humanity.

ACTION ITEM:

This one is really going to push your limits...and it's really going to be fun. Each day this week I want you to go up and introduce yourself to a total stranger. Tell them you are doing a self-help and discovery program called The Last Year of Your Life, and that today's assignment is to ask a total stranger to share with you what their dream or ambition was when they were a kid. Ask them this exact question, "What did you dream about becoming or doing when you grew up?" and then just listen to them and try to connect with their dream or personal ambition. Make a note about each one:

DAY 1:

DAY 2:

DAY 3:

DAY 4:

DAY 5:

DAY 6:

DAY 7:

EXERCISE:

Make a conscious choice to be kind to one person each day this week.

1.

2.

3.

4.

5.

6.

7.

Week 22. Overcome Fear and Personal Barriers

"Inaction breeds doubt and fear. Action breeds confidence and courage.
If you want to conquer fear, do not sit home and think about it.
Go out and get busy."
–Dale Carnegie

In this program, we simply don't have time for the limiting belief of fear.

You've probably heard the expression "paralyzed by fear." That's exactly what fear does to humans and other animals—it stops you dead in your tracks. Well, we're all going to be dead soon enough, so in this program we conquer fear using a simple technology I learned from Tony Robbins in March of 2001.

I've used this technology many times since then, but one time really stands out in my mind because I was able to overcome my fear and earn a profit of almost two hundred thousand dollars.

It was January of 2003 and I was surfing the internet one day when, simply on a whim, I typed in www.ForSaleByOwner.com

Up came a real estate listing site that I had never been to before or even heard of. The site had a box in which you could enter a zip code, so I did, and up came a list of eleven properties for sale, one of which was priced at eighty thousand dollars. I clicked on it.

It turned out to be a graffiti-covered shack in a not-so-nice neighborhood. I looked at the pictures, and then I clicked on the "contact owner" link. Up popped an email.

I was about to start typing a message to the owner when I suddenly became paralyzed by fear. My fingers literally froze on the keyboard. Then I heard the voice of fear.

It sounded very familiar. It was the little, tiny voice in my head that I had heard a billion times in my lifetime.

The voice was my own.

Knowing my vulnerabilities as well as I did, the voice spoke with total precision and economy of words. The voice said ten words to me in total: "Who are you to be buying a graffiti-covered shack?"

That was the dastardly voice of fear, and that was all the voice had to say to literally immobilize my fingers.

But luckily, in the very next instant, I heard the voice of Tony Robbins in my head, and he said, "If you're afraid, you must."

Half as many words.

Ten times as powerful.

"If you're afraid, you must."

Say that out loud to yourself.

I did. Right then, I said it out loud to myself: "If you're afraid, you must."

Five words.

As the beginning of a brief yet key conversation with myself that I actually had, sitting my desk chair, I said, "If you're afraid, you must."

Then I said, out loud, echoing the voice of fear, "Yeah, but who am I to be buying a graffiti-covered shack with a mind toward tearing it down and building a new house? I've never built a whole house before!"

It was true. At that point in my life I had bought a cosmetic fixer in a slum neighborhood, fixed it up, and rented it out to a Section 8 tenant (on government assistance) and at that very moment in time I had one worker in my fiancé's backyard digging a trench that would become the footing for a room addition. That was the sum total of my construction experience: a cosmetic fixer and the footing trench.

By that time my fingers had left the keyboard and had sunk down onto my thighs as these thoughts flew through my mind.

And again the voice of fear: "Who am I?"

Asking me that question for which I had no good answer.

All I had was some hokey piece of Tony Robbins "technology."

"If you're afraid, you must." I said it again, out loud, then I lifted my hands off my thighs, put my fingers back on the keyboard, and typed an email that began a chain of events in which I outbid some other guy for that shack and paid eighty-two thousand dollars for a vintage 1926 structure with a hole in the floor where the toilet used to be and the words "fuck you" painted on the front door by a vandal.

I put the paperwork together, applied for, and got a construction loan from Indy Mac Bank—God bless that bank! Then I tore down that shack and built a three-bedroom, one-bath, brand new house in its place.

When I sold that house I profited almost two hundred grand. I took that money and rolled it over into a piece of land in one of the best neighborhoods in the city, and I'm in the process of getting the permits to build my dream house on that piece of land.

One day I will be living in a multi-million-dollar dream house because of five words.

"If you're afraid, you must."

ACTION ITEM:

Any time you want to take action during this Last Year of Your Life, if you find yourself paralyzed by fear, I want you to use the five-word technology.

I'm not talking about doing anything stupid, like stepping in front of a bus. I'm talking about when you want to take positive action and do something courageous in your life—when you are definitely going to come up against the barrier of fear. It will sound like an all-knowing version of your own voice, and it will be telling you that you're not enough, or that you don't have the experience, the education, enough money, or a million other excuses covering up the real culprit: fear.

When that time comes, that's when you will hear my voice, and I will be saying, "If you're afraid, you must."

Then your voice of fear will answer me. And that's when it will be your turn to pick up the conversation.

That's when it will be your turn to be courageous, to conquer your fear, to take a stand for progress in your life, to boldly go where you have never gone before.

Let me know how it turns out.

I am rooting for you.

Week 23. Unclutter Your Life & Eliminate Procrastination

"The more you have, the more you are occupied.
The less you have, the more free you are."
– **Mother Teresa**

I am a Virgo. It all starts and ends right there.

When I was 12 years old I got my very own bedroom. It wasn't long after I moved into that room that I started clearing out the clutter and crafting it into the paragon of order and neatness that I needed to create so that I could function to maximum effectiveness and with maximum peace.

This decluttering process involved taking huge boxes full of my mom's books (which were piled high on my shelves, taking up my precious space) down to the library across the street and donating them. Man, was my mom pissed!

She was even more pissed when one day a few months later she discovered that I had gone into the kitchen closet and decluttered the top two shelves. That also involved giving away all the dusty books that were crammed and clustered in there, and even though they were cook-books she never used, she'll still bring it up as a point of resentment to this very day.

It just got to the point where I could not take it any more.

I wanted to find something, and all that clutter was too much in my way and too much for me to bear. It had to go.

You see, along my journey I've learned something profound from a friend of mine named Lorie Marrero, the author of "The Clutter Diet" – and that is this: every single piece of clutter is a psychic tentacle holding you down, weighing you down, burdening you mind, spirit and soul.

If you want to lose weight, clutter will hold you back from achieving your goal.

If you want to accomplish anything great in this life, clutter will stop you, or at least slow you down significantly.

If you want have great relationships with people, clutter will prevent that. It's a barrier that you put up to keep people out.

There was a man on my men's team who we all thought was full of shit. He talked a good game, but you could tell there were holes and cracks in every story. He told us once that he wanted to clean up the clutter in his house, and we said we would hold him to that. Six months later, when I was the team leader, I decided we would go to inspect the premises.

He refused. "If I have to quit this team, I will," he stated with all seriousness.

But as much as he resisted, that's exactly how much I persisted.

Eventually we had to get in there. It took another month of constant pressure before he finally let us into his 1 bedroom apartment.

He had worked hard during that month (and mind you, that was after 6 months of alleged clearing that had gone on before I started to pry.) I had seen worse. We could walk around, there was more than just little pathways between stacks, but not very much more. It was a shame, too, because if he could've just let go, we could have cleaned out that apartment in a single day's time. But he could not let go.

He just could not. He was afraid. He was attached. He was addicted to his stuff. And all that stuff was consuming him.

Here was a man who always talked about wanting a relationship with a woman. But how can you have a relationship with someone when you won't let anyone into your house? How can you let anyone into "your life" if they can't even come over to visit for a cup of tea?

I wish he would've just abandoned all the pretense and the fantasy and the wanting to look good in everyone's eyes (including his own) by repeatedly coming back to his stated goal of being able to date and have a relationship. There's no way it could've ever happened with any sane person.

I guess the bottom line is that everything comes down to priorities. Is your stuff your priority, or is your soul? Do you care more about the things, or the experiences? Do you want a collection, or do you want people in your life?

Ultimately, you have to get into action and start throwing stuff away.

If you haven't touched it in a year, just touch it one more time, on the way to the trash can. Then be rid of it forever.

Feel the lightness and joy of eliminating clutter from your life. Experience the great sensation of being in action by getting your stuff out of your own way.

ACTION ITEM: Tackle a clutter situation in your life and obliterate it. Take an hour, take a day, take a weekend, and really accomplish something positive for your life. If you think that war zone of a garage is not weighing you down, you are wrong!

MY TOP 3 CLUTTER PROJECTS:

1)

2)

3)

I have 20 free videos for you to watch on the subject of clutter and creating more time to deal with your clutter at www.DeclutterNow.info

Procrastination is the other side of the same coin. You procrastinate, so you don't have to make the tough choices, and thereby choose without choosing.

If you are still procrastinating, you need to go back and review Week 8 – take responsibility for your actions and your life.

ACTION ITEM:

Make a list of any important things you've been procrastinating and do them all this week!

1)

2)

3)

4)

5)

How does it feel to have knocked those out? _____

_____

_____

Week 24. Align Yourself with Your Life's Purpose

"Focusing your life solely on making a buck shows a poverty of ambition.
It asks too little of yourself. And it will leave you unfulfilled."
–Barack Obama

How do you know you are doing what you are "meant" to be doing on this Earth? How do you know if what you are doing is the "right" thing for you?

Do you actually have a true purpose for your life?

These are major questions for a lot of people. I know they have been for me.

Most of all, I have often wondered, How do I know I'm doing something that I'm really supposed to be doing with my life?

There are some people who toil and toil and toil for years until they "make it" and suddenly become an "overnight success." Other people achieve a grand measure of success immediately.

Joe Pesci tried to make it in the movie business for fifteen years with hardly any results until Robert Deniro got him the part of Jake Lamotta's brother in Raging Bull, and then he won an Oscar.

But do you have what it takes to toil ignominiously for more than a decade, and still somehow know that you are the one who is going to cure cancer? Do you have that kind of inner fortitude?

Or are you more like Kirstie Alley, who according to legend, came out to Hollywood in her early thirties and immediately landed a starring role on Cheers?

Or like President Obama, whose meteoric rise in politics is well-known by all?

In my personal experience, if you are in alignment with what the universe "wants" from you, or what you are truly capable of, you will get very clear signals of success that will become visible almost immediately.

When I was a fourteen-year-old kid I saw a sign in the cafe window across the street from my apartment building on 23rd Street. I walked in and immediately went to work as a dishwasher that same day. In less than four months I was preparing the orders as a "counter man," and just a few months later I was a waiter making two hundred dollars each weekend throughout tenth and eleventh grades. That's a lot of money for a kid back in 1980 and '81!

I applied to the Wharton Business School, with no connections, no family money (they gave me 50 percent need-based financial aid so that I could attend) and got in with an early decision acceptance.

In college I was an average student until I discovered the Entrepreneurial Management department, where I got an A in every single course I took.

After college I started doing an "entrepreneurial art project" called "trash art." I was making sculptures out of trash by sealing garbage in plastic containers and signing my name on them. Three weeks after I made my first sculpture, I was in the Los Angeles Times, on LA's KCBS News, and on national television as a guest on Fox's Late Show.

I counted up the circulation and audience figures of all the newspapers, magazines, radio and TV shows that did stories about trash art and calculated that 100,000,000 people heard my environmental message about the global trash crisis through that work in the span of only two years. I made it into Time magazine and the Wall Street Journal, but I threw that all away when I got seduced by the movie business and spent the next ten years trying to make it as a screenwriter and a movie star.

I put more effort and did more to become a movie star than just about anyone ever did, and yet I failed to make it. By the end of my "career," I put together a vampire movie that I had written, was producing, and raised the money to shoot as a Super-16mm movie. I was on an island off the coast of California for a day and a half with a cast and crew of seventy-five people, starring in the movie, and then it all exploded when the director stupidly instructed a set dresser to cut some leaves for set dressing from a protected wetlands area and we got thrown off the island.

Not to be deterred, I convinced the director to use our remaining twelve thousand dollars to shoot the movie again on Mini-DV, and this time we went back to the island without permits to shoot the scenes which were set on a boat off the coast. We used beaches and parks on the mainland to double for "on the island" scenes, and when it was all shot and in the can, the director broke up with his wife, moved to Canada, then packed up the tapes and hid them in an attic somewhere in Canada before leaving on his boat to circumnavigate the globe—never to be heard from again.

I should have been a movie star. I wanted to be a movie star so much. I tried so hard to bend the moon and stars to my will. But it was not meant to be. That was not my true life's purpose.

When I was a kid I starred in every school play. Robert Downey Jr. and Jon Cryer both went to my junior high school, and look at them today. They were no better than me. I am convinced that if it was my true life's purpose to become a movie star, that's what would have happened immediately for me.

I finally got distracted from movies because I started making so much money selling raw butter and cream. And not only did I "instantly" start making a bunch of money from that business, but I also soon was working with the very top people in the gourmet restaurant industry. Within a year of entering the butter business, my clients were many of the top chefs in America.

It truly seems to me that the way the world works is this: if you're doing what you're supposed to be doing, you will know it very quickly. If you're just working in a job—not fulfilling your "true destiny" or potential—you can just muddle along for years with nothing ever happening in your life.

The question is, are you willing to take the risks and make the changes to explore other avenues and opportunities until you find your true calling? Or are you going to spend the remaining weeks of The Last Year of Your Life taking home that same old paycheck, because that's what you've always done?

ACTION ITEM:

1) Write a sentence about the experiences in your life that have brought you some immediate success:

     a)_____

     b)_____

     c)_____

2) Write a sentence about the experiences in your life that have yielded you nothing but struggles, hardship, and frustration for prolonged periods of time.

     a)_____

     b)_____

     c)_____

3) Is there any episode in your life where you feel you should have kept trying? What did you give up on too soon?

_____

4) What career have you always secretly longed for but never had the guts/money/time to try?

_____

_____

Week 25. Give Yourself Permission To Have Fun Every Day

"It's only when we truly know and understand that we have a limited time on
Earth -- and that we have no way of knowing when our time is up -- that we
will begin to live each day to the fullest, as if it was the only one we had."
– Elisabeth Kubler-Ross

My wife and I were recently down in Herradura and Jaco, Costa Rica, doing
some due diligence work on a real estate investment we've been working on
for two years. We were down there to see what the action was like nowadays
where we're planning on investing—what the business climate is like, are
there as many tourists, etc.

I didn't have a hotel reservation for our last night, and I decided to book a
room in a beachfront mini-resort about twenty minutes south of "our" towns.
Even though it wouldn't be a work experience related to our investment, I
wanted to take a little time for us.

The next morning I really wanted to get an early start back up to San Jose
because I wanted to stop and take a last swim at my favorite beach and still
be able to return the rental car without any late penalty. The contract clearly
stated in English, "There will be extra charges for extra hours."

But after breakfast I noticed that the tide was super low. The high-tide line was less than fifty feet from our hotel room, but it probably took us five minutes to walk all the way down to the water's edge at this low tide, and am I glad that we did!

There was practically nobody on this beach. The sand was hard-packed and flat enough that a guy rode a 100cc motorbike along the middle of the beach. Here and there a few pelicans soared and swooped and dove for fish.

We walked toward the sun for about twenty minutes, splashing in the hot tide pools and wavelets, and marveled at the two guys catching two-foot-long yellowtail tunas with simple wire lines and hooks in the surf. Each of them had two big yellowtails just lying on the beach above the tide line.

My wife said, "This is the most beautiful beach I've ever been on in my life." I was amazed by this, as my wife has been on more than her fair share of gorgeous beaches—with me in Tahiti during our honeymoon, while she was producing movies in Thailand, and throughout her beach-filled life.

The most beautiful beach I've ever been on... I can't tell you how much pleasure it gave me to hear her say that.

We turned around and, on the way back, more and more tide pools were actually massaging our feet with hot water. You could take a bath in that water, it was so hot.

By now the fishermen had covered up their catches with sand to keep them from cooking in the sun.

As we turned away from the water's edge and started walking back to our hotel, a small, single-engine plane flew up along the coast. He was so low, maybe thirty-five feet above the beach, right above the fishermen and where we had been walking.

"Wow," I marveled, looking at the plane. "You can't do that in the United States." For the first time in my life I got a feeling of how free and exhilarating it must feel to pilot a small plane.

By the time we checked out and got on the road, it was already almost the time I had intended to be leaving my favorite swimming beach for the drive to the airport. I hate late charges!

So as we drove around the curve and took in the view of Jaco Bay, I already began lamenting my missed swim.

But fifteen minutes later, as we approached the beach turnoff, I impulsively swerved and started speeding down the narrow private road to the coast.

I parked the car and made a beeline for the water. Man, that water was gorgeous. Clear, blue, calm, uncrowded swimming heaven. I went up the beach to the end of the cove in fifteen minutes, and then I dived down and selected a small piece of white coral off the bottom and put it in my pocket.

Fifteen minutes back and then I picked up a black rock on the beach and slipped that in my pocket as another keepsake, something I only do on rare occasions when I have an amazing time—for example, I took home two shells from an amazing beach on my Tahitian honeymoon.

I drank a cold glass of tap beer at the beach bar, and then we hit the road.

On the way back to San Jose International Airport I tried not to drive too aggressively or let the impending late fees get me down. Making it on to the plane was going to be close, too.

By the time we got to the airport, the sky had clouded up with a black storm of thunderclouds. Gone was the beautiful sunshine of the morning, and in its place it was raining gatos and perros!

The car rental guy did not charge me a late fee. We made our plane with plenty of time to sample the free cups of Costa Rican coffee in the shops near the gates, and to daydream about how wonderful that Monday morning walk on the beach and my bonus swim were.

They were the standout memories of that whole trip—all because I made sure that we took the time to smell the roses.

What it all comes down to is a feeling—that you are worth it; that you deserve to enjoy yourself, that you are entitled to those precious moments and memories.

Taking time to smell the roses is about getting every bit of the sweet nectar of life. Make that extra effort to get those last drops of ambrosia—many times that's where you will find life's greatest joys just waiting for you.

ACTION ITEMS:

Each day this week I want you to stop and smell the roses. Write about the events, but more importantly, write about how the action of stopping to smell the roses makes you feel.

Day 1)

Day 2)

Day 3)

Day 4)

Day 5)

Day 6)

Day 7)

Week 26. Understand The True Foundation Of All Personal Power

"Character is power; it makes friends, draws patronage and support,
and opens the way to wealth, honor, and happiness."
–John Howe

Think about a steel beam. That's one of the strongest things in the world, right? Unless it has a little crack, or becomes degraded in some way. Then it can break under normal stresses and strains.

Remember the bridge collapse in Minneapolis a couple years ago? A steel bridge crumbled and killed a bunch of people. An entire eight-lane steel bridge—boom, gone in a second!

How could that happen to a steel bridge?

The steel beams somehow had their integrity compromised, through tiny cracks and imperfections. Once they ceased to have perfect integrity, the steel bridge collapsed. (If you type "I–35W Bridge" into Wikipedia you can watch a security camera video of the bridge actually going whoosh!)

If that could happen to a steel bridge that normally would support eight lanes of traffic, what do you think the impact of any lack of integrity would be on your own little, tiny, fragile life?

You're not made out of steel! All you are is flesh and bones—a bundle of fragile, organic matter powered by Taco Bell and Diet Coke, constantly churning with emotions, often times blowing with the wind like a little leaf.

Take a look at the fissures in your personal integrity, and let's examine what and where they are costing you.

How about the lack of integrity in your diet? Are you eating real, whole foods packed with nutritional goodness, or are you consuming food-like products marketed at you by giant corporations like McDonalds? Is that real iced tea, or pseudo? Is that an actual piece of fish, or a fish-stik? (Yes, with a k.)

How about your word; are you keeping your commitments when you speak, or are you just flying off at the mouth to tell people what they want to hear?

Most importantly, are you letting yourself get away with little lies and broken promises to yourself? Are you out of integrity with your own self? What do you think is the price of broken commitments to yourself? How many thousands of times have you told yourself you're going to do something, but haven't? You know full well when you've broken a commitment to yourself, which means you know that you are a liar. How does the fact that you know that you are a liar impact your self-esteem?

This is the place where integrity has the most value and the most cost: for your own self. Every time you are out of integrity, you know it, and it reduces your sense of self-worth.

Every time you cheat, lie, or steal, you know that you are doing it, and it costs you.

Every time you do the right thing, you know that you are doing the right thing, and it builds you up. It may cost you a few pennies or bucks in the moment, but those are investments in your self-esteem, in your sense of moral correctness, and in your integrity.

One time last year I cashed a check at the bank and the girl gave me one too many hundred-dollar bills. I caught it, and I made her recount. When she realized the mistake, she was so incredibly grateful to me for being honest, because bank tellers have to pay for any shortages out of their own money. It cost me a hundred bucks. But it was worth thousands!

Integrity is like a bank account. When you compromise your integrity, you draw down on your integrity balance. When you do the right thing, whatever that is, you make a deposit in your sense of moral correctness.

ACTION ITEM:

This week you are going to keep a record of all the integrity choices you make. Good and bad. Right or wrong. You know what they are; you know when you are doing it; and you are going to be honest and write them down.

Record ten integrity choices in the margins of this page, and put a + or a – next to each one, according to whether it was a deposit into your integrity bank account, or a withdrawal.

At the end of the week, add up the plusses and the minuses and give yourself a grade from –10 to +10. Write about how you feel.

INTEGRITY SCORE: _____

How I feel about my own level of integrity: _____

_____

_____

_____

_____

_____

_____

_____

_____

"He that respects himself is safe from others.
He wears a coat of mail that none can pierce."
–Henry Wordsworth Longfellow

EXTRA CREDIT: Take a picture of yourself today "on the job," and paste it here.

Week 27. Appreciate Your Life Experience

ex·pe·ri·ence   [ik-speer-ee-uhns] noun, verb,-enced, -enc·ing

—noun

1. a particular instance of personally encountering or undergoing something: My encounter with the bear in the woods was a frightening experience.
2. the process or fact of personally observing, encountering, or undergoing something: business experience.
3. the observing, encountering, or undergoing of things generally as they occur in the course of time: to learn from experience; the range of human experience.
4. knowledge or practical wisdom gained from what one has observed, encountered, or undergone: a man of experience.
5. Philosophy. the totality of the cognitions given by perception; all that is perceived, understood, and remembered.

—verb (used with object)

6. to have experience of; meet with; undergo; feel: to experience nausea.
7. to learn by experience.

—Idiom

8. experience religion, to undergo a spiritual conversion by which one gains or regains faith in God.

> "Experience is one thing you can't get for nothing."
> – Oscar Wilde

I'll tell you what I know about experience: there are some experiences in life that absolutely change a person.

You go into a set of circumstances as a certain kind of person, and you come out on the other side a completely changed human being.

The Last Year of Your Life is one of those experiences that is going to change you.

ACTION ITEM:

Write down some of the experiences in your life that have changed you.

1) _____

2) _____

3) _____

Something else I know about experience is this: just the fact that you're alive is no guarantee that you are going to experience anything.

In order to have experiences in life, you have to put yourself out there into positions where you are vulnerable.

The price of experience is risk, or pain, or regret, or a chunk of your ego.

Look back on those three experiences that changed you and made you who you are today; were they situations where you risked something? Were they circumstances where you had to pay some kind of price?

All those lessons you learned as a result of taking the risks that provided you with the real experiences of your life—those are the things that have formed you into the person you are today. And in the weeks that remain in The Last Year of Your Life, you are going to try to jam as many more experiences in as you possibly can.

Because that is where the juice is.

In the doing.

In the being.

In the actions you take to have the experiences.

ACTION ITEM:

Pick one of the CPR results that has been most elusive for you, and take massive action this week to make it happen.

Put yourself into the fire, so that you have a major, serious, life-changing experience this week in the process of getting one of your results.

You are going to change this week.

You are going to have a profound life experience this week.

You probably know which result is most scary for you. Go for it! Go out there and change your life this week.

Experience what it feels like to transform.

Become a butterfly.

Week 28. Flip A Switch & Create Real Courage to Change

God grant me the serenity
to accept the things I cannot change;
courage to change the things I can;
and wisdom to know the difference.
Living one day at a time;
Enjoying one moment at a time;
Accepting hardships as the pathway to peace;
Taking, as He did, this sinful world
as it is, not as I would have it;
Trusting that He will make all things right
if I surrender to His Will;
That I may be reasonably happy in this life
and supremely happy with Him
Forever in the next.
Amen.
–Reinhold Niebuhr

Sometimes change just happens for us, or to us. You can get hit by a bus and your life is totally changed without you having to even think about it for one iota.

Other times we have to deliberately set out on a path to bring a change into our lives. That takes courage.

If you want to quit smoking, or to get out of a relationship, or to find a new job, or to begin a new exercise routine—all of this requires courage.

I remember when I was twenty-eight years old and wanted to quit smoking. I was at the point where I would wake up in the morning and cough and cough and cough. Yet I was addicted to the nicotine, and I loved the ritual of smoking, and I'd been doing it for almost ten years—it was a huge part of my personal image of who I was. As a writer, there was a part of me that worried about the impact of quitting smoking upon my writing. Would I still be able to write?

So that's where courage came in. Courage is feeling fear and doing something anyway.

I felt genuine fear about what my life was going to be like—personally, professionally, and in a sense spiritually—if I quit smoking. But I needed to make that change; my body needed it and was demanding it, so I did it despite my fear.

I've done a lot of performing over the years too—plays, karaoke, television shows and interviews, radio interviews, and even some big business meetings. These all involve stage-fright to a certain extent. I get a nervous feeling in my stomach, and sometimes I even worry about staying in control of my bladder! (Seriously.) But I always manage to just move forward and do it anyway.

Every time I've felt fear and done it anyway. Every time. I have never said, "I can't do this," and backed out of something. Never. I always go through with things.

I guess that's courage. At the time it's happening, though, to me it has always felt like I was just doing what had to be done. That's courage: feeling fear, doing what has to be done, and just moving forward through fear and past fear. That's courage. And that's what it takes to change.

ACTION ITEMS:

Look back on your life to moments when you felt fear and did it anyway.

Make a list of those moments of courage. Your first kiss, your first job application, your first day of high school, buying a car, negotiating with a mechanic or contractor, getting up on stage to get your diploma—these might all be moments of courage.

1)_____

2)_____

3)_____

4)_____

5)_____

6)_____

7)_____

8)_____

9)_____

10)_____

Did you know you were that courageous? I hope you had the stick-to-it-ive-ness to fill in all ten of those lines, because everyone has at least ten moments of courage in their life, and you deserve to recognize yourself for them.

Do you see any patterns? Do you remember ever feeling fear and doing something anyway? Can you identify those moments of courage in your life?

Do you see how the mantra "If you're afraid, you must" is a formula for courage? If you just use that mantra every time you feel fear, you will be living a life controlled by courage, not fear.

What kind of life do you want to live? Circle one: Courageous or Fearful

"Do not fear to step into the unknown, for
where there is risk, there is also reward."
–Lori Hard

Extra Credit: Pick the scariest thing on your CPR and paste in a picture of yourself doing it this week. If there's nothing "scary" on your CPR, do something "courageous."

Week 29. Perfect Your Time Management Skills

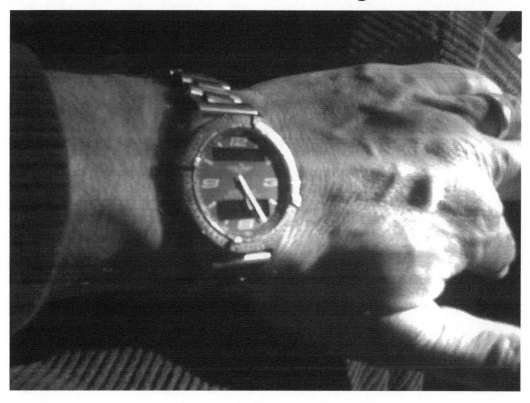

"Delay always breeds danger, and to protract a great design is often to ruin it."
-Miguel de Cervantes

I have always been very conscious of time.

Even when I was a kid, I always bought myself black, plastic Casio watches that were water-resistant, had calculators and stopwatches and other gizmos on them, and (most importantly) glowed in the dark so I would always know what time it was in the middle of the night.

Today I like my watches just as much, but I like them to be better watches, such as Breitling, Tag, Ebel, or Rolex. I appreciate time enough to invest in fine timepieces for myself and my wife.

As a native New Yorker, I've always been very concerned with making good time whenever I travel. There's so much traffic and potential for delay in New York that time is a widespread concern among most New Yorkers I know. It also has bred a deep need to avoid waiting on long lines—what a total waste of time.

I love to have a good time. In fact, I have parties and good times on my CPR every year because I want to make sure I have enough good times every year to compensate myself for all the hard work I put in.

The time of my life was during my honeymoon in Tahiti. That was an amazing time—seventeen days of nothing but time for swimming, feasting, drinking, loving, and good times.

These days my perspective on time is focused by The Last Year of Your Life—with the looming deadlines of the ticking countdown clocks on the front page of the website—and the looming global "deadline" of December 21, 2012, when the whole world is supposed to come to an end.

For some reason, I always thought I was going to die when I was twenty-eight. That's the year I had a major motorcycle accident; I totaled my Honda Interceptor when I had a blowout of my front tire at sixty mph on the 10 Freeway outside downtown Los Angeles.

All of a sudden I found myself traveling in slow motion as my bike skidded in front of me, on its side, and I slid on my butt in the middle of five lanes of heavy traffic.

After what seemed like an eternity, everything came to a stop. I stood up and felt my arms and legs for broken bones. There were none. I had a couple minor scratches on my hands, but otherwise I was relatively unscathed by my brush with death. I had cheated death and transformed my own ticking clock.

But still the urge to stay on top of time has remained with me.

What about you? What's your relationship to time and your own day of reckoning? Do you ever wonder whether you are going to make it to the very end of The Last Year of Your Life, or will your final moments come sometime before the finale of your program?

Is this spooky for you? The producer of Coast To Coast told me she thought the whole idea of living The Last Year of Your Life was kind of scary. It is.

But that's the reality of the situation. Nobody knows how much time they have. For all you know, you could be dead tomorrow.

ACTION ITEM:

This week I want you to be five minutes early for everything.

Week 30. Access The Power Of What You Already Know

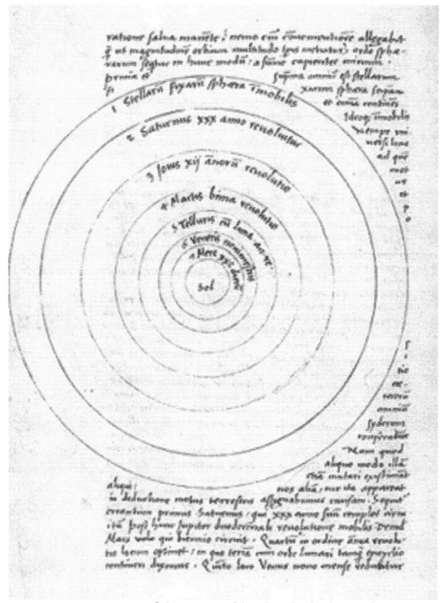

A page out of Copernicus' book, which changed
everyone's concept of common knowledge.

What do you know?

What do you think you know?

For thousands of years, all the greatest minds in the world thought that the
sun revolved around the Earth.

People were put to death for advancing the idea that the EarthEarthEarth revolved around the sun. They were killed for that heresy!

One notable exception was Louis XIV, the Sun King, who thought that the world revolved around him. That was okay, because he was the king.

Nicolas Copernicus was lucky enough to die very soon after publication of his book *De Revolutionibus Orbium Coelestium* (*On the Revolutions of the Heavenly Spheres*) in 1543.

After that book was published, the radical shift from a geocentric to a heliocentric cosmology was a serious blow to Aristotle's science and helped usher in the scientific revolution—a whole scientific revolution from just one little adjustment in general knowledge!

So now let's bring this all down to something very personal for you.

Before The Last Year of Your Life, death was probably not on your radar. Now you have twenty-two weeks to go until you die. Have you truly absorbed that knowledge yet?

Are you living as if you have twenty-two weeks left to live?

Pull out your CPR and write down the four most important results you want to achieve before this life is over.

1)_____
2)_____
3)_____
4)_____

I want you to knock out all four of them so that you really feel value for these last few weeks and you can reformulate your knowledge of what is possible for you.

How are you going to make it happen?

Change your context and you change the rules.

"Knowing others is wisdom; knowing yourself is enlightenment."
–Lao Tau

Week 31. Eliminate Your Fear Of Death

"Nothing in the world is as certain as death."
– Jean Froissart 1359

The first time I saw a dead body was when I was twelve years old.

I was a delivery boy for the florist across the street from my apartment building, and one afternoon they sent me down to the funeral parlor on 21st Street with a big basket of flowers.

I had no idea what I was in for.

The funeral parlor was right across the street from my junior high school, and a block north of my old elementary school, so I had been tangentially aware of the place for several years but I had never paid it any mind.

Until that day.

On that day I entered the dimly lit vestibule with my arms wrapped around the big basket of flowers, and my eyes fitfully scanned the empty room.

To my relief, a thin, older man in a dark, pinstriped, three-piece suit came out and asked, "Can I help you?"

I looked at the card pinned to the cellophane wrapping and said, "Paglioli?"

The thin man motioned to an open doorway.

I timidly walked towards the portal and stepped into the salon.

Thirty-five feet away was a very white, very old man lying peacefully in a casket.

There was a table near the coffin with another basket of flowers on it, so I quickly deposited mine beside those and made a hasty exit.

When I emerged into the daylight outside the funeral parlor, I gulped lungfuls of fresh air and lamented the fact that nobody tipped me.

It would be eighteen years until I saw another dead body: my grandmother's.

I loved my grandmother more than anyone in the whole world. She had passed away in the hospital, of pneumonia, at the age of eighty-two. We were there with her near the end, but she died during the night. The last time I saw her alive, she was breathing laboriously with her tongue hanging out of her mouth—long and thick like a horse's tongue.

By that point my sweet granny had become an animal, struggling to remain alive, sucking air on instinct.

When the limousine pulled up to the cemetery, a representative from the graveyard said they needed a family member to identify the body.

My brother and I got out and walked over to the hearse.

They opened the rear door and slid off the lid to the pine box.

She looked tiny inside there. I nodded somberly and said, "That's her."

There have only been two others that I've seen—my father and my mother-in-law, and I'll spare you the stories. Forty-four years of life on this planet, and I've only personally witnessed four dead bodies.

Considering how many people die every day, that number seems like a tiny amount, wouldn't you say?

Our society tries to insulate us from death. We cover up the dead with a sheet. We zip them into body-bags. We box them up in coffins.

Nobody wants anybody to have to see the faces of death. It's too disturbing.

Yet it's part of the circle of life—a very real part of it. It's an extremely powerful part of it, if you can harness that power for yourself.

ACTION ITEMS:

1) Write about the first time you ever saw a dead body. How old were you? Where were you? What were you thinking about? _____
_____
_____

2) Go to a funeral or a cemetery this week and contemplate life and death. Write about your thoughts and emotions. _____
_____
_____

3) "For a warrior, every day is a good day to die." Write about your reaction to this statement. _____
_____
_____

4) Would you be ready to die today? Why or why not? _____
_____
_____

"Every man dies. Not every man really lives."
–William Wallace

Week 32. Create Unstoppable Personal Power Being Real

"Weak people cannot be sincere."
– La Rochefoucauld

You are coming to a point in your life where you are going to make a drastic shift about tolerating bullshit in your life. And that point is...

Now.

The first thing you have to realize about bullshit is that it comes from you.

All the bullshit in your world emanates from you as the source.

Do you think Oprah has any bullshit in her life?

Do you think President Obama has any bullshit coming his way?

From just the way those people look at you, you know they are coming from total authenticity, and as a result they get back total authenticity.

People try to please them, authentically.

People try to do their very best for Oprah and President Obama because they expect that of people. And they expect people to be real with them.

So how does a person "get real" and "be real"?

A lot of it has to do with being in alignment with your true life's purpose. That is a subject dealt with in-depth in another chapter, so I'm not going to go into it too much here other than to say that when you are aligned with your true life's purpose, the energy of authenticity will simply flow out of you.

Because it stops being about your ego.

The main reason why people come across as full of shit is because it's not really them talking; it's their ego.

The ego is concerned with one thing: looking good.

Do you think Oprah or President Obama spend one second thinking about or trying to look good? Or are they just doing their thing? Are they just being themselves, in the moment, making history, making their own personal history?

Trying to be right all the time is not being real.

Trying to look good is not being real.

Trying to do anything is not being real. It's inauthentic by definition.

You can either try, or you can do.

When you are brushing your teeth, are you trying to brush your teeth, or to look good brushing your teeth, or to be something you aren't? No, you're just brushing your teeth. You're just "being" a man or woman brushing their teeth.

ACTION ITEM:

Go in the bathroom and brush your teeth. Right now. Take note of how you are being. Feel the way you feel inside your skin while you are brushing your teeth. That's the real, true, authentic you.

That's the way you want to be all the time; not trying to be anything more than who you really are. Not trying to look good. Just getting the job done. Just being real.

How does that feel? Compare and contrast who you are being and how you feel when you are just being you with how you felt in the past when you were on a bad first date, or in a job interview, or in any circumstance from your life where you were trying to look good.

How I felt brushing my teeth: _____
_____

How I felt when I was trying to look good: _____
_____

EXERCISE:

This week I want you to be real with seven people. First we'll start you off with the easy stuff: being real with strangers.

Be yourself. Bring it on. Be fully present in the moment, just being you. Be the best you. Look people in the eyes. Smile if you feel like it. Don't if you don't. Be authentic in the moment by not trying to be anything. Just be a person. Be right there in the moment with another person. Do that with four strangers and write a short paragraph about each.

1) _____
_____
_____

2) _____
_____
_____

3) _____
_____
_____

4) _____
_____
_____

Now comes the hard part: to be real with people you care about.

They are going to notice something is different, because you are going to be different.

Instead of worrying about how you look, or any other ego-related activity, you are just going to be. You are going to be the best possible you, or the worst, but whatever you are going to be, it will be the real you, completely in the moment. Not trying, just being.

Of course you are going to write about it:

5) _____

_____

_____

_____

6) _____

_____

_____

_____

7)_____

_____

_____

_____

ACTION ITEM:

For the next few weeks I want you to make a concerted effort to not try to look good. Just forget about looking good. Just be yourself. Try to avoid looking in the mirror. Don't worry about your appearance.

Trust that whatever you do is enough.

Trust that however you show up will be good enough.

Live as though your real, actual, true self is just perfect.

Week 33. As Good As It Gets

"People living deeply have no fear of death."
–Anais Nin

There's the fantasy, and then there's the reality.

In our dreams, we are winning Academy Awards, flying on private jets everywhere we want to go, and are married to a Playboy bunny or Richard Gere (depending on your gender or orientation).

But the reality of your existence is that you are now thirty-three weeks into The Last Year of Your Life, and chances are that this moment—yes, right here and now—is as good as your life is ever going to get.

Take that in.

I have been pushing you, and you have been pushing yourself for all these many months, and there's quite possibly some different energy in your life right now, you've probably made some changes, and you could be on your way to bigger and better things...

But what if you're not? What if this moment is the best energy and spirit you're ever going to have?

What if this level of achievement and these relationships with the people in your life are the culmination—the singular moment that you will look back on as being The Very Peak Moment of Your Whole Entire Life?

How do you feel about that? _____

_____

_____

_____

Is there any area of your life that you wish you could do over? And if so, what would you want to do differently? With whom would you want to do it?

_____

_____

_____

ACTION ITEM:

I want you to express your gratitude for all the wonderful things that you have in your life at this moment. Complete the following statement: I realize that my life at this moment is as good as it's ever going to get, and right now I am most grateful for...

_____

_____

_____

_____

_____

Week 34. Become A True Leader

"Leadership and learning are indispensable to each other."
–John F. Kennedy

You didn't know that this program was a leadership seminar, did you?

It is.

All this while you have been taking important steps to gaining the greatest type of leadership, and that is to be able to lead yourself.

During these past thirty-three weeks you have been leading yourself through this process, and since you have made it this far I can honestly say that you are doing one heck of a fine job.

Seriously.

Do you understand the level of commitment and follow-through that is involved with staying up on a program of this nature for thirty-three weeks? It's huge!

Congratulations.

This success in leading yourself is a clear indicator that you have what it takes to be a leader in other areas of your life. You have what it takes to be a leader of other people.

The first step in this week's leadership mini-seminar is our mantra:

"I am a great leader, and I will be proving it over and over every day for the rest of my life."

I want you to repeat that mantra five times a day, every single day, for the rest of The Last Year of Your Life.

Write it down five times right now:

_____

_____

_____

_____

_____

If you just repeat that mantra five times every day for the rest of this program, you will undoubtedly become a better leader. There's no doubt about that. If you've done any serious work with mantras already, then you know that to be true. So do it.

You see, while you are in this program, I want you to take advantage of all the beauty that is inside of you. And part of that is growing into the leader that you should be in your life. It is by leading in your life that you will gain the greatest sense of personal satisfaction, because like Frank Sinatra used to sing in the song, you will have done it your way. And nothing feels as good as that.

ACTION ITEMS:

Write down the names of some leaders whom you admire:

_____

_____

_____

_____

_____

_____

_____

Think about some of the great leaders you have known or known of in your lifetime. Write down some of the qualities that you think most embody the spirit of leadership: (I'll start you out with some examples.)

    1) Calm
    2) In control
    3) Balanced
    4) Giving
    5) Focused
    6) Clear
    7) Determined
    8) Empowering
    9) Spiritual
  10) Humble
  11) Enthusiastic
  12)
  13)
  14)
  15)
  16)
  17)
  18)
  19)
  20)

To me, one of the most important aspects of being a leader is producing results. Results are the bottom line, and they are how we keep score as leaders.

I encourage you to create a CPR for an upcoming event or meeting that you are going to lead, and to put down the results you want to achieve from this leadership experience.

Like in your personal CPR, there are two kinds of results that a leader will achieve: concrete and ethereal. Write down ten to fifteen concrete results, and four or five ethereal results. From those results, you will determine what the Purpose of that event is, and from there you will find a Context to support you in leading the way to those results and that purpose.

Don't be shy; just jump right in and create the CPR for whatever event or meeting you will be leading in the next week. It could be something at work, or with your friends or kids. Whatever it is, just turn the page and do it now.

CPR for _____

CONTEXT:_____

PURPOSE:_____

_____

RESULTS:
1)
2)
3)
4)
5)
6)
7)
8)
9)
10)
11)
12)
13)
14)
15)
16)
17)
18)
19)
20)

Next, I want you to create an agenda for that event, and for every result on your CPR, you should have an agenda item that will support you in achieving your results.

For example, one of your results should always be "My participants and I had fun!" (Hint: write that down if it's not already part of your results.) So you need to put some sort of fun activity in the agenda so that you accomplish the result. This could be a game, or a song, or just an opportunity for participants to tell jokes. Something fun.

Next, I want you to think about that event you will be leading as an official part of The Last Year of Your Life Program, and as such, it's going to be special; it's going to be a privilege for you to lead this event. I want you to treat it as something sacred. Even in the way you drive to the meeting, I want you to hold it as something very special.

Before that meeting starts, I want you to envision what is going to happen, how it's going to happen, and what the overall feeling of the event will be. It's the leader's responsibility to create a vision of what's going to happen.

Trust your gut.

Don't be a slave to your agenda. A lot of times the best stuff happens that's not even on the agenda, so allow that to be if it presents itself.

If you're lucky and you execute well as a leader, your meeting will have some surprises in it; people will feel a bit uncomfortable; they will have fun; they will experience emotions; they will speak personally; they will gain new tools that will help them in life and in the task at hand. The meeting will provide some "Aha!" moments, include some real belly laughs, and create moments of true intimacy. Doesn't that sound like the kind of meeting you'd want to attend?

If you led a meeting like that, wouldn't people be clamoring to attend more of your events? That's what's possible for you if you put care and attention into planning your meetings.

Keep this in mind: Life is a game. Change your context and you change the rules.

Strive for excellence, not perfection.

You can choose to be successful. You can choose to be happy. Life can be that way.

Every single day you want to grow and have fun, and you want to lead others in the direction of growth and fun too.

"We are what we repeatedly do."
– Aristotle

Week 35. Get Passion In Your Life On A Cellular Level

pas·sion [pash-uhn] noun
1. any powerful or compelling emotion or feeling, as love or hate
2. strong amorous feeling or desire; love; ardor
3. strong sexual desire; lust
4. an instance or experience of strong love or sexual desire
5. a person toward whom one feels strong love or sexual desire
6. a strong or extravagant fondness, enthusiasm, or desire for anything: a passion for music
7. the object of such a fondness or desire: Accuracy became a passion with him.
8. an outburst of strong emotion or feeling: He suddenly broke into a passion of bitter words.
9. violent anger
10. the state of being acted upon or affected by something external, esp. something alien to one's nature or one's customary behavior (contrasted with action)
11. (often initial capital letter) theology
a. the sufferings of Christ on the cross or his sufferings subsequent to the Last Supper
b. the narrative of Christ's sufferings as recorded in the Gospels
12. archaic. the sufferings of a martyr.

"Passion is the genesis of genius."
–Anthony Robbins

Passion makes our life full and juicy.

Passion is what moves men to accomplish great things.

And it leads nations to war.

Where do you have passion in your life? What are you passionate about?

What drives you and gets your blood boiling? _____

What gets you out of bed in the morning? _____

What do you rush places to do? _____

Who do you feel passionately about? _____

What causes or movements have you felt passionate about during at some point in your lifetime? _____

Don't go any further until you fill in all those blanks.

Seriously.

A life without passion is not a full life. Life without passion is merely survival. Passion is the key ingredient for success.

You need to be able to be passionate about something in order to progress with the rest of this program.

ACTION ITEMS:

1)Take personal responsibility for your life and for your passion. You are the only person who can fan the flames of passion in your life. It's completely up to you to create the circumstances, habits, and desires that will become passion.

2)Look for passion and find it. Be proactive and challenge yourself to create or develop passion in your life. Look for the positive. Seek out tiny new kernels of passion and cultivate them.

3)Plan for passion. Make time to pursue your personal interests and help them to flower into full-blown passions. What could you do to nurture your budding passion? How could you encourage some tiny growth spurts into full-fledged blooms of passion?

4)Decide you are going to be passionate about something. Whatever it is, commit to a program or plan of action around that personal interest and follow through with it. Passion can be instinctual, but it can also just as easily be the result of concerted efforts, study, and development. Decide on what your passion will be and make it happen.

5)Fan the flames of passion. Look back over your efforts and congratulate yourself on your wins and achievements in the realm of your passion. Develop an attitude of caring and personal enthusiasm.

6)Don't overdo it. As with many things, less can be more. Go for it, be active about your passion, but don't overdo it or else you'll burn out.

7)Be curious and interested in the world. There is so much amazing art, literature, food, architecture, and natural beauty all around us. Allow the world in which you live to inspire you and evoke passion.

8)Stay positive. Avoid people and situations that bring you down and douse the flames of passion within you.

9)Share your passion. Include someone you love or care about in your activity or passion play. There is power in numbers, and you want to spend time with people who either share your passion or who can be encouraged to join in your passion.

10) Get juiced about passion. Read these amazing stories about people who say they are very passionate:

http://www.experienceproject.com/groups/Am-Very-Passionate/263

EXTRA CREDIT: Take a picture of your passion or something you feel passionately about TODAY, and paste it in here:

Week 36. Understand & Access True Spirituality

"Spirituality is a domain of awareness."
–Deepak Chopra

I am not a religious person.

But I am a spiritual person.

Spirituality is what brought me back to the men's team.

And spirituality is the gift that I wish to give to you with this program.

A spiritual gift.

It took me a long time to understand what spirituality is.

I was raised in one of the big four religions, and I never felt an ounce of spirituality from any religious service. Of the millions of prayers I said over the years, perhaps I felt something tingly from three or four of them.

It wasn't till I hit my thirties when I finally got an idea of what spirituality was. At that time it came from sexuality. Intense sexuality. And it came from the attainment of being fully present in the moment with another human being who was also fully present in the moment.

For the first time in my life I really felt what it meant to be alive, and for me that was spirituality. And I really only had it with women.

Until I took the Men's Weekend. In the Weekend, there's a room full of between 150 to 200 men who are all very present in the moment. And there are some extremely spiritual experiences in that room among those men.

That's what makes the Weekend so amazing and special for so many men: the experience of true spiritual moments.

And then the Weekend is over, and for many men, those spiritual moments become just a memory.

They were for me—until I got onto a great men's team.

On the team level, I have had the thrill of experiencing spiritual moments many, many times. I refer to these moments as "the Magic."

They are moments when time slows down, the air gets very still, and every person in the circle can feel a special energy and connection with the power of the universe.

Clarity of mind gives you the ability to see to the heart of the matter.

All of a sudden you just know things.

You know the truth.

That's what keeps me coming back for more, week after week: the Magic.

I realize now that the Magic is present whenever you are fully present in a moment and everyone else you are with is also fully present in the moment.

If you are with one person, if they are fully present in the moment you will feel something special from your interaction.

If you are in a group, it's harder to achieve because more people have to be fully present in the moment in order to get the Magic. If one person is out of the moment, this will probably kill the Magic.

Battle can be very spiritual for this very reason.

Crisis moments are often spiritual experiences, and the spiritual intensity can be so great that it bonds people together forever. (Watch this video http://cnn.com/video/?/video/living/2010/01/14/natpkg.miracle.hudson.couple.cnn about the couple that got married after they survived the crash on the Hudson.)

Sports activities can be spiritual. Consider the high that runners get, or the special feeling that teammates get when they play games together, or the bond that boxing opponents feel for each other after they've spent the evening pummeling each other senseless. All of these spiritual moments are the moments people remember for their entire lifetimes.

How great would it be to live an entire lifetime in the thrall of spirituality?

It is possible.

Easy? No.

Possible? Yes.

It's all about staying present in the moment, being present in the moment with people you are with, and being mindful of the preciousness of every second of life. This can be an acquired way of being. You can create this type of spirituality for yourself any time you want.

ACTION ITEM:

We are going to activate our spirituality right now.

a)Spirituality by yourself: I want you to go into a stairway and walk up three full flights of stairs. When you get to the third landing, I want you to stop, close your eyes, listen to your heart beating in your chest, and feel the blood coursing through your veins.

Then open your eyes and look around at everything. Take in the colors and the shapes and the way the light feels. Lick your lips and taste your saliva.

How does it feel to be alive and using all your senses? Do you feel any of the Magic?

b)Spirituality with another person: You need to go someplace quiet with that person, maybe the woods, or a deserted park, or a beach at night. Remove a layer of clothing so that you can feel the air or the chill of the night—not because you're naked, just because you are underdressed.

This is about using your senses, activating your sense of smell, touch, taste, hearing, and sight. Get physical with that person: wrestle a little with them, not to pin them, but just to get both of you feeling your bodies, feeling your muscles, feeling the moment.

Then when you stop wrestling, look into that person's eyes and be fully present with them in the moment. Don't let them look away. Just be present and be there with them. Don't talk for a minute. Just be there. Be there and feel the Magic.

Week 37. Experience "Joie de Vie" (The Joy Of Life)

Joy of Life - Henri Matisse 1906

"Joy is not in things, it is in us."
-Richard Wagner

The Joy of Sex.

The Joy of Cooking.

Joy to the World.

Almond Joy.

Jump for joy.

Ode to Joy.

Joie de Vivre... the Joy of Life.

A little kid can experience joy simply by jumping in a puddle.

A dog experiences true, profound joy when his master comes home at the end of the day.

A baby accesses the miracle of joy when you toss it up in the air—just not for too long.

What does it take to get you to joy? Is it that piece of chocolate cake? Is that really joy?

Is it a new car? Is a new car really what you need to feel joy?

What about a morning in the church pew? Does that stoke you to joy?

I know that for me, the first time I dive into crystal-clear, warm, blue ocean water at a tropical beach—that first time for sure—that rush of salty, warm wetness gets me to joy. It must be like a symbolic return to the womb for me, because I love it so much.

This week I want you to connect with true joy. This week I want you to go after it and hunt it down and make it happen for yourself.

If not now, when?

Make a list of the things you try, and rate them on a scale of one to ten:

1)
2)
3)
4)
5)
6)
7)
8)
9)
10)
11)
12)
13)
14)
15)

Week 38. Take a Stand For Something Big In Your Life

"Don't believe that winning is really everything.
It's more important to stand for something.
If you don't stand for something, what do you win?"
–Henry C. Blinn

As you approach the final three months of The Last Year of Your Life, I want you to think about what you would be willing to die for.

Is there anything you care enough about that you would take a stand and make the ultimate sacrifice?

It's funny: you look at the Lincoln Memorial and you see that because he took a stand, he gets to sit.

But seriously, think about the stand that Abe Lincoln took, what he was able to accomplish, what it cost him, and what it earned him.

Remember, the Confederate States of America actually seceded from the Union. He had to fight a war to break up their new country and bring them back into the United States of America.

You think Iraq is a bad situation for the United States? Think about the fact that half the country didn't even want to be part of our country anymore. They quit the country! They tore up their passports, printed new money, got a new flag, and elected a new President. And they started a new army.

How many people up North do you think were gung ho about going down to the South and killing their cousins and brothers and friends who lived below the Mason-Dixon Line?

They looked just like us. They spoke the same language. They had been us. But now we had to fight them and kill them.

Would you want to do it?

Lincoln stood for something clear. He had made a famous speech on June 16, 1858; it was known as his "House Divided" speech. Here is an excerpt that clearly lays out what Lincoln stood for: (In the first line he quoted Jesus.)

"A house divided against itself cannot stand."
I believe this government cannot endure, permanently, half slave and half free.
I do not expect the Union to be dissolved; I do not expect the house to fall; but I do expect it will cease to be divided.
It will become all one thing or all the other.
Either the opponents of slavery will arrest the further spread of it and place it where the public mind shall rest in the belief that it is in the course of ultimate extinction, or its advocates will push it forward till it shall become alike lawful in all the States, old as well as new, North as well as South.

Good old Abe Lincoln stood for a United States of America, where every man, woman, and child was free. He stood for it and led us through one of the bloodiest and most horrible wars this country ever fought—where every single American was killed by another American—until he brought the Union back together. And we're still together to this day. Because Abe Lincoln took a stand.

So what do you stand for? _____

_____

_____

Week 39. Develop Genuine Connections with Strangers

"Some people come into our lives and leave footprints
on our hearts and we are never ever the same."
–Flavia Weedn

These days I find myself having genuine connections with people even when I'm filling my car's gas tank down at the ARCO station.

It can happen without speaking a word.

It can happen in the few moments of a shared glance.

It can happen in an airport, in the supermarket, on the subway, or in an elevator.

I was in Las Vegas last week, and when I got on the elevator one morning there was a couple already in there, on their way down to the casino. I said, "How's everybody doing this morning?" And I looked at them in the eyes. We had a very real and genuine conversation for those thirty-one floors we spent together. I really, genuinely cared how they were doing, and they responded with genuine interest in me and how I was too.

That's the thing about connecting with people; if you make an effort, they will make an effort.

It all comes down to the simple tool of assuming the rapport. If you assume the rapport of having a genuine connection with a person, and be real—be present with them in the moment and put yourself out there—people will always respond in kind because they are hungry for genuine connection.

Our society can be so hurried, impersonal, superficial, and cold, so when a person feels the warmth of a genuine person coming at them, they respond.

Earlier during that same trip, I left my wife with the bags while I went to the front desk of the hotel to check in. When I came back, she was deep in a conversation with a man from Pittsburg who was in town for a family reunion. We talked for a few minutes about cellphones, family, good places to eat, and when it was time to go our separate ways that man shook my hand four times. I'm not kidding.

Now part of it is definitely because I have a beautiful and charming wife. But aside from that, what I try to do with everyone I meet these days is to look the person in the eye when I talk to them—to listen to them and really try to hear what they are saying and understand what they are getting at.

I try not to hurry through conversations or interactions, but rather, to let them unfold in a natural course.

And last but certainly not least, I try not to make any judgments about the person. When I look at a man, he's just a man. A woman is just a woman.

ACTION ITEM:

This week I want you to go out and have a genuine connection with at least one person each day and make notes about them.
1)_____
2)_____
3)_____
4)_____
5)_____
6)_____
7)_____

Week 40. Appreciate Each Moment of Your Life

"This—this was what made life: a moment of quiet, the water falling in the fountain, the girl's voice...a moment of captured beauty.
He who is truly wise will never permit such moments to escape."
–Louis L'Amour

Life is made up of moments, one after another, always moving, always passing, always the briefest instances of time.

Moments.

I remember when I was a little five-year-old kid being taken by my mom to a birthday party. I remember not wanting to go, and picking the gift we had brought out of the big bag of presents all the kids picked from. I picked it because I knew what it was, and because it was the one I had brought, and when an adult found out that I had picked the present I had brought, they told me to put it back in the bag and select again. I did. But I don't remember what that present was. Just that moment.

I remember the moment in little league baseball when my brother hit an easy grounder to me, a star player, and the ball went right under my mitt and between my legs...going to the Atlantic Beach Hotel fire with my grandfather at two in the morning and watching it burn down...catching butterflies on the beach with my brother and grandmother one year when there were millions of Monarch butterflies...

I remember singing the part of Tony in West Side Story as an eighth grader... walking to school in the morning as a ninth grader, listening to Ziggy Stardust on my walkman every day, and arriving in front of the school building with sweat on my brow...making up my mind to go to Wharton... getting a 100 on the New York State Geometry Regents and being accused of cheating by my math teacher...getting an early decision acceptance to Wharton...

Swimming in the lake at Tripp Lake Camp when I taught sailing the summer before starting college...going skinny-dipping one time late at night when I thought nobody was watching...ripping a flowering limb off a magnolia tree and putting it in my dorm-room sink like a vase...smoking cigarettes and hanging out on the front steps of "The Castle" (my fraternity)...the dinner where Digby Baltzel told us we were the best fraternity because we were merit-based...

Dinner with Nora after the Spring Formal junior year...interning at Swiss Bank for Coach Mike, going to work in the summer in my Armani suit...summer classes in Florence...motorcycling across America on my Interceptor...

Making phone calls and smoking cigarettes on the balcony of Jim Morrison's old apartment in Venice Beach...putting my foot through my surfboard during a huge swell...my one-hundred-dollar movie premier in Beverly Hills...

Bradley Method birthing classes...the doctor pulling my daughter out of her mother's c-sectioned stomach...driving the director of Cirque de Soleil down to John Wayne Airport from LAX in my Yellow Cab...

Cold winter nights on my boat listening to Jewel and reading Angela's Ashes...barbecuing on the dock...my 1971 Ford Bronco...writing the Hell's Angels story...staring in movies that never got finished...getting Spike Lee to give me his hat...my grandfather dying...my parents' divorce...writing my first book with Tommy Leonardi...adapting Roger Zelazny's novel into a screenplay for my friend and her partner...my grandmother dying...

The Men's Weekend...my first 40# order of raw butter showing up via Fedex...my first jars of oysters when I started going raw...modeling jobs...trips to Vegas...meeting my wife in a parking lot...my first men's team...my first fixer...my first tear-down...building my first house...my wedding...my honeymoon in Tahiti...my first Warhol...becoming president of JLP Foundation...Sicily, Rome, Mykonos...my father's death, and my mother-in-law's, in the span of three weeks...

Being elected team leader...creating The Last Year of Your Life...Coast to Coast with George Noory...ABC15 Phoenix...today.

I just took you on a guided tour of my whole entire life, in just over a page: forty-four years in 540+ words. That's life. It goes by just that fast. It may take a long time each day to get to Miller Time, but when you start looking back on the decades, they go ripping by at warp speed.

Think about the past thirty-nine weeks. I bet they've been packed with tons of good stuff, and each day has been a treasure, hasn't it? But those are 273 days you can cross off your final allotment for this go-around on planet Earth —especially if you've been living fully, been fully engaged in this process, been all in.

One minute you are a kid at a birthday party, seemingly the next minute you are standing at your parent's memorial service...or lying in a hospital bed praying to God to let you get well and live more of a healthy life.

I often wonder where I'll be and what I'll be doing when I realize, This is it, it's all over.

ACTION ITEMS:

1) Look back on your own life and write down some of the highlights.

a) A childhood memory: _____

b) A grade school memory: _____

c) A high school memory: _____

d) A young adult memory from your twenties: _____

_____

e) A highlight from your thirties:_____

_____

2) Write a few sentences about the first time you ever saw a dead person:

_____

_____

_____

3) Get a watch or a timer and take a five-minute walk around the block or neighborhood. When the five minutes are up, write down a shorthand version of all the thoughts you had during those five minutes:

_____

_____

_____

_____

_____

_____

_____

_____

_____

_____

_____

_____

_____

_____

_____

_____

Week 41. Unburden Yourself From Your Sins and Transgressions

"The beginning of atonement is the sense of its necessity."
–Lord Byron

The first time I did this exercise I was astounded by its power.

When I "invented" it, I had an idea in my mind about what I was going to confess, but when I got to the moment, something else entirely came up.

This process has its roots in the Catholic ritual of confession, where a person goes into a little booth and confesses their sins to a priest, who then gives them a penance to do and grants them absolution.

Not being a Catholic, I never had this available to me. But I had a feeling it would be good for me in some way.

The day came when I found myself paired up with a buddy, and it was my turn to go. That's when I got to the heart of it.

When my father was very ill and we knew the end was near, both my brother and I spent the last few days with him in the intensive care unit of Sloan Kettering Memorial Hospital. It took a few days for my father to puff up and finally succumb to the complications of his various system failures. It was a grueling, grinding descent towards death.

He died on a rainy Saturday afternoon in November, and although we'd been with him for many, many hours leading up to that moment, when the time came for him to actually pass out of this world, my brother and I were having lunch and drinking Guinness at a pub on First Avenue.

We got back to his room and a couple of nurses were busy over his body.

They asked us to wait in the hallway, and we knew what had gone down while we were out.

I felt like crap. Like I had him down. Like I was a bad son.

And I told all of this to my buddy. He was an ex-Marine, and a very thoughtful and sensitive person.

He pondered the situation a few moments, and then he said, "Your father's death was his death. You weren't there because he didn't want you there. If he had wanted you there, you would have been there."

That really struck a chord for me. My father was a very private person. I knew in that moment that my buddy was right. If my dad had wanted us to be there when he died, we would've been there. But he didn't, so we weren't.

ACTION ITEM:

Team up with your buddy, either on the phone, via webcam, or in person, and confess your "sins" to that person. Be daring and get out what your soul really needs to get rid of. If your buddy has anything to say, take it in. If not, just let it go. Let it all go—as much as you can get rid of.

When you're done confessing, it's your turn to be there for your buddy. Just let them talk, and take in whatever they have to say. When they're done, if you feel any urge to respond to what they've told you, let the truth come out from deep inside you. Allow your inner wisdom to bubble up and flow. Don't think about it; just speak what the universe wants you to say.

Week 42. Make Amends to All People You Have Injured

"Mistakes are part of the dues one pays for a full life."
–Sophia Loren

We all screw up. That's part of being alive. But making amends for your mistakes is part of becoming a real human being, and not just another animal.

Animals go through life with no conscience, no remorse, and no thoughts about how to better themselves.

This program is all about taking your life to the next level, and one of the most important ways you are going to do that is by making amends to people you have injured in your lifetime.

Last week you got to confess your sins, so you've had some time to think about the horrible things you've done in your lifetime.

Now I want you to make a list of the people you screwed over and injured, and a brief note about what you did to them.

1)_____
2)_____
3)_____
4)_____
5)_____
6)_____
7)_____
8)_____
9)_____
10)_____

If you need more room, write in the margins.

ACTION ITEMS:

With every single one of those people, you're going to make amends. It's a six-step process.

1) Tell them that you know what you did, and that you are taking responsibility for what you did.

2) Say you're sorry for what you did. Be genuine and straight up with the person, tell them why you did it, and promise them that you'll never do it again.

3) If possible, make up for what you did. If it's at all humanly possible to do something to make the situation right, then make it right. If you can't make it 100 percent the way things were before you screwed the person over, then do as much as you possibly can to set things straight.

4) Don't be pushy. They don't have to accept your apology; they don't have to even talk to you if they don't want to. All you can do is try, and be sensitive to the fact that you may have totally burnt the bridge, so don't be too pushy.

5) Offer to help them with anything they may need help with. Again, be sensitive to the fact that they may not want you in their life at all, let alone to make you privy to what's going on in their life, so they may refuse your offer. But if you can help them with something, do it.

6) If they're open to it, move forward with the relationship as a fresh start.

Week 43. Give Your "Last Lecture" & Become A Great Speaker

"If I could only give three words of advice, they would be, 'tell the truth.' If I got three more words, I'd add: 'All the time.'"
–Randy Pausch

Randy Pausch (Oct 23, 1960 – July 25, 2008) was a Professor of Computer Science, Human-Computer Interaction, and Design at Carnegie Mellon University in Pittsburgh, Pennsylvania, and a best-selling author, who achieved worldwide fame for his speech The Last Lecture at Carnegie Mellon University, after being diagnosed with pancreatic cancer and having only a few months to live.

If you have not seen his speech, you can watch it right now (and you should) athttp://www.youtube.com/watch?v=ji5_MqicxSo

The Last Year Of Your Life is your own personal opportunity to get all the benefit of a terminal disease like pancreatic cancer, without any of the pain, suffering and heartache.

I want you to look over your life and come up with the most important lessons you learned, the most significant insights you realized, the most profound meaning you've discovered. Turn the page and write it down, as if this was your only opportunity to share this stuff with your best friend or your kids.

Go.

(I'm going to make it a little easier for you with this simple format...)

What I really want you to know about what I've learned in my life is...

1) _____

_____

_____

_____

_____

_____

2) _____

_____

_____

_____

_____

_____

3) _____

_____

_____

_____

_____

_____

And always remember to ..._____

_____

Week 44. Empower Yourself With Genuine Gratitude

"Gratitude is the fairest blossom which springs from the soul."
–Henry Ward Beecher

You could have been a slave...

Or a soldier ripped to ribbons on Omaha Beach...

Or a serf during the Dark Ages...

Or a starving child in Ethiopia...

Or stillborn...

Or illiterate...

Or mentally impaired...

Or you could've been hit by a bus and killed that time...

Or tossed in a dumpster when you were a baby...

You could've been any of those things, but you weren't. If you are reading these words, you are indeed one of the most fortunate people on the Earth. You've had the leisure time and money enough to spring some on this fifty-two-week personal endeavor, and I congratulate you for that.

Now I want you to congratulate yourself for the bounties of your life.

Every day this week I want you to write down at least six things that you're grateful for. You can write more if you want to. This is a gratitude diary:

1) _____ _____ _____

_____ _____ _____

2) _____ _____ _____

_____ _____ _____

3) _____ _____ _____

_____ _____ _____

4) _____ _____ _____

_____ _____ _____

5) _____ _____ _____

_____ _____ _____

6) _____ _____ _____

_____ _____ _____

7) _____ _____ _____

_____ _____ _____

Week 45. Resolve All Outstanding Personal Issues

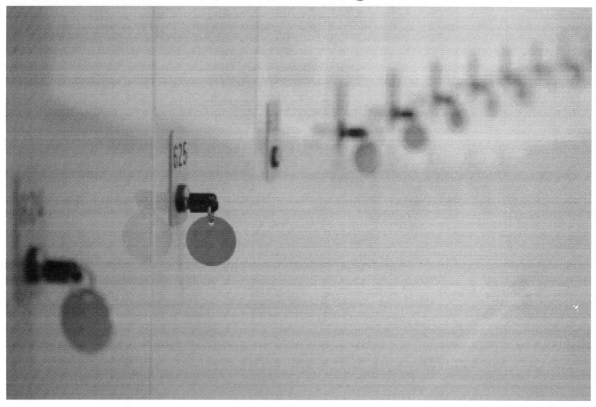

"I never told my father I loved him before he died, and I have a lot of
issues about that. They're all swimming around in my head, in my heart,
unresolved, and in a way it felt fitting to dedicate the film to him."
–Gary Oldman

Have you noticed only eight weeks remain in The Last Year of Your Life?
That's not a lot of time. But it's still a considerable chunk of days.

It's actually twice the lifespan of a housefly. Imagine that. A housefly has to
live its entire life in a maximum of just thirty days.

You've got sixty days! Man, those flies are jealous of you! (Everything is a
matter of perspective.)

The point is to make those days count. And since we're getting down to the
end of days, you need to be making the best use of the little time you've got.

You need to use that time to make sure you've resolved any personal issues,
so that when you lie down to die, you can feel like there's nothing major left
over that you wish you could've taken care of.

What does that mean? When you were just reading the previous paragraph, you probably had some ideas flashing through your head. What were they?

Maybe they are CPR items that you still haven't gotten to?

Maybe they are stuff you weren't expecting, and they're coming at you now straight out of left field?

I don't know; this is a custom program just for you, and your personal issues are your very own unique circumstances.

But what I do know is that you've got enough time to go after at least one of them, if not all three. And I want you to do it.

This week you've got to go out and conquer at least one of those unresolved personal issues.

How are you going to do it? By getting uncomfortable. By stretching out of your everyday lifestyle. By going for it. That's how.

Is it going to be easy? No.

Is it going to be fun? Could be.

Are you going to be glad you made it happen? Definitely.

Now get moving! Do it! You don't want to have any regrets when it's time for you to die.

ACTION ITEM:

Write down the top three unresolved personal issues in your life.

1)_____

_____

2)_____

_____

3)_____

_____

Week 46. Your Last Will and Testament

LAST WILL

OF

MICHAEL JOSEPH JACKSON

I, MICHAEL JOSEPH JACKSON, a resident of the State of California, declare this to be my last Will, and do hereby revoke all former wills and codicils made by me.

I

I declare that I am not married. My marriage to DEBORAH JEAN ROWE JACKSON has been dissolved. I have three children now living, PRINCE MICHAEL JACKSON, JR., PARIS MICHAEL KATHERINE JACKSON and PRINCE MICHAEL JOSEPH JACKSON, II. I have no other children, living or deceased.

II

It is my intention by this Will to dispose of all property which I am entitled to dispose of by will. I specifically refrain from exercising all powers of appointment that I may possess at the time of my death.

III

I give my entire estate to the Trustee or Trustees then acting under that certain Amended and Restated Declaration of Trust executed on March 22, 2002 by me as Trustee and Trustor which is called the MICHAEL JACKSON FAMILY TRUST, giving effect to any amendments thereto made prior to my death. All such assets shall be held, managed and distributed as a part of said Trust according to its terms and not as a separate testamentary trust.

If for any reason this gift is not operative or is invalid, or if the aforesaid Trust fails or has been revoked, I give my residuary estate to the Trustee or Trustees named to act in the MICHAEL JACKSON FAMILY TRUST, as Amended and Restated on March 22, 2002, and I direct said Trustee or Trustees to divide, administer, hold and distribute the trust estate pursuant to the provisions of said Trust, as hereinabove referred to as such provisions now

exist to the same extent and in the same manner as though that certain Amended and
Restated Declaration of Trust, were herein set forth in full, but without giving effect to any
subsequent amendments after the date of this Will. The Trustee, Trustees, or any successor
Trustee named in such Trust Agreement shall serve without bond.

IV

I direct that all federal estate taxes and state inheritance or succession taxes payable
upon or resulting from or by reason of my death (herein "Death Taxes") attributable to
property which is part of the trust estate of the MICHAEL JACKSON FAMILY TRUST,
including property which passes to said trust from my probate estate shall be paid by the
Trustee of said trust in accordance with its terms. Death Taxes attributable to property
passing outside this Will, other than property constituting the trust estate of the trust
mentioned in the preceding sentence, shall be charged against the taker of said property.

V

I appoint JOHN BRANCA, JOHN McCLAIN and BARRY SIEGEL as co-Executors
of this Will. In the event of any of their deaths, resignations, inability, failure or refusal to
serve or continue to serve as a co-Executor, the other shall serve and no replacement need be
named. The co-Executors serving at any time after my death may name one or more
replacements to serve in the event that none of the three named individuals is willing or able
to serve at any time.

The term "my executors" as used in this Will shall include any duly acting personal
representative or representatives of my estate. No individual acting as such need post a
bond.

I hereby give to my Executors, full power and authority at any time or times to sell,
lease, mortgage, pledge, exchange or otherwise dispose of the property, whether real or
personal comprising my estate, upon such terms as my Executors shall deem best, to
continue any business enterprises, to purchase assets from my estate, to continue in force and

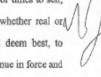

Page 2

pay insurance premiums on any insurance policy, including life insurance, owned by my estate, and for any of the foregoing purposes to make, execute and deliver any and all deeds, contracts, mortgages, bills of sale or other instruments necessary or desirable therefor. In addition, I give to my Executors full power to invest and reinvest the estate funds and assets in any kind of property, real, personal or mixed, and every kind of investment, specifically including, but not by way of limitation, corporate obligations of every kind and stocks, preferred or common, and interests in investment trusts and shares in investment companies, and any common trust fund administered by any corporate executor hereunder, which men of prudent discretion and intelligence acquire for their own account.

VI

Except as otherwise provided in this Will or in the Trust referred to in Article III hereof, I have intentionally omitted to provide for my heirs. I have intentionally omitted to provide for my former wife, DEBORAH JEAN ROWE JACKSON.

VII

If at the time of my death I own or have an interest in property located outside of the State of California requiring ancillary administration, I appoint my domiciliary Executors as ancillary Executors for such property. I give to said domiciliary Executors the following additional powers, rights and privileges to be exercised in their sole and absolute discretion, with reference to such property: to cause such ancillary administration to be commenced, carried on and completed; to determine what assets, if any, are to be sold by the ancillary Executors; to pay directly or to advance funds from the California estate to the ancillary Executors for the payment of all claims, taxes, costs and administration expenses, including compensation of the ancillary Executors and attorneys' fees incurred by reason of the ownership of such property and by such ancillary administration; and upon completion of such ancillary administration, I authorize and direct the ancillary Executors to distribute, transfer and deliver the residue of such property to the domiciliary Executors herein, to be distributed by them under the terms of this Will, it being my intention that my entire estate

Page 3

shall be administered as a unit and that my domiciliary Executors shall supervise and control, so far as permissible by local law, any ancillary administration proceedings deemed necessary in the settlement of my estate.

VIII

If any of my children are minors at the time of my death, I nominate my mother, KATHERINE JACKSON as guardian of the persons and estates of such minor children. If KATHERINE JACKSON fails to survive me, or is unable or unwilling to act as guardian, I nominate DIANA ROSS as guardian of the persons and estates of such minor children.

I subscribe my name to this Will this ___ day of _____, 2002.

_____
MICHAEL JOSEPH JACKSON

On the date written below, MICHAEL JOSEPH JACKSON, declared to us, the undersigned, that the foregoing instrument consisting of five (5) pages, including the page signed by us as witnesses, was his Will and requested us to act as witnesses to it. He thereupon signed this Will in our presence, all of us being present at the same time. We now, at his request, in his presence and in the presence of each other, subscribe our names as witnesses.

Each of us is now more than eighteen (18) years of age and a competent witness and resides at the address set forth after his name.

Each of us is acquainted with MICHAEL JOSEPH JACKSON. At this time, he is over the age of eighteen (18) years and, to the best of our knowledge, he is of sound mind and is not acting under duress, menace, fraud, misrepresentation or undue influence.

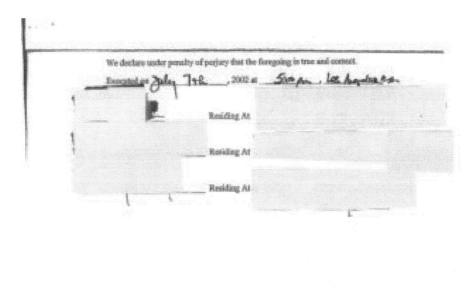

We declare under penalty of perjury that the foregoing is true and correct.

Executed on *July 7th*, 2002 at *5:16 pm, Los Angeles, Ca.*

_____ Residing At _____

_____ Residing At _____

_____ Residing At _____

Page 5

> "For what is it to die but to stand naked in the wind and to melt into the sun?
> And what is it to cease breathing, but to free the breath from its restless tides,
> that it may rise and expand and seek God unencumbered?"
> –Kahlil Gibran, The Prophet

Now that you've read the will of a person who could afford to hire the best attorneys to write it for him, type up your own will. If you want any more instructions on what to do and what not to do, go to this link and read what they have to say: http://www.essortment.com/all/willlastwilla_rnew.htm

When you are done, have a friend be your witness and sign their name to make it official.

Week 47. Appreciate The Accomplishments of Your Entire Life

Yes... John Adams is a high benchmark, and probably an unfair measure of comparison for you, me, and most everyone we know. But read his obituary, and on the page that follows, write your own. Think back over your life and commemorate the best moments in a few paragraphs that could sum up your existence. Good luck!

ALBANY ARGUS & CITY GAZETTE.

ALBANY, TUESDAY MORNING, JULY 11, 1826.   [VOL. XIII—NO. 165.

[From the N. Y. Statesman.]

The venerable JOHN ADAMS, late President of the United States, one of the ablest and most efficient advocates and supporters of the Revolution, an original signer of the Declaration of Independence, a patriot and statesman, whose career was full of honor, whose life, services, talents and virtues, were the pride and glory of the nation, expired at his residence in Quincy, Mass. on the 4th day of July, at the advanced age of 92. His death on the Jubilee Anniversary of that Independence which, FIFTY YEARS before, nearly at the same moment of time that his spirit left its earthly tenement, he pledged his fortune, honor and life, to support, is one of the most remarkable coincidences in the history of man.

Had he been permitted by the BEING to whom he owed his existence, who endowed him with great talents, and kept him in that course of irreproachable virtue and honor which has rendered his memory immortal, to select the time when his disembodied spirit should take its flight, he would probably have chosen the very moment when a whole nation were employed in celebrating the glorious result of patriotism, when his name, and those of his compatriots, was upon the lips of ten millions of people, and the voice of gratitude and joy was resounding throughout the whole of the American Republic.

BOSTON COURIER OFFICE,
Wednesday, July 5—one o'clock.

DIED, at his residence in Quincy, at 6 o'clock in the afternoon of the 4th of July, the Hon. JOHN ADAMS—in the 92d year of his age.

Annexed will be found the proceedings adopted by the authorities of Massachusetts, on learning the death of JOHN ADAMS.—The few particulars that marked this last scene are given in the Boston papers: the most remarkable one is, that having been for some days failing,—"On the Jubilee "of Independence, his declining faculties "were roused by the rejoicings in the me-"tropolis. He inquired the cause of the "salutes, and was told it was the fourth "of July. He answered, 'it is a great "and glorious' day.' He never spake "more. Thus his last thoughts and his "latest words were like those of his whole "life, thoughts and words which evinced "a soul replete with love of country and "interest in her welfare."

OBITUARY OF _____ Born:_____ Died:_____
(Write in the 365th day of your program)

_____
_____
_____
_____
_____
_____
_____
_____
_____
_____
_____
_____
_____
_____
_____
_____
_____
_____
_____
_____
_____
_____
_____
_____
_____
_____
_____
_____
_____
_____
_____
_____

Week 48. Understand the Meaning of Your Life

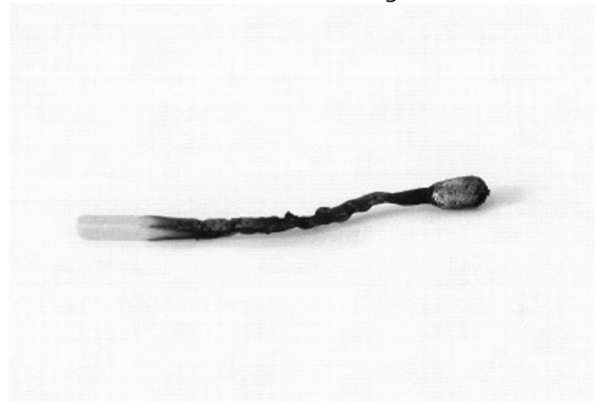

"Life is without meaning. You bring the meaning to it.
The meaning of life is whatever you ascribe it to be.
Being alive is the meaning."
–Joseph Campbell

When I was twenty years old, I went on a trip to Caracas, Venezuela for spring break. I know, it's an unusual place to go for spring break, but I'm an unusual kind of guy.

I was still smoking cigarettes in those young days of foolishness and seeming immortality, and one afternoon while I was out for a walk, I stopped on a street corner and lit a cigarette with a match.

It was the middle of the day and the beach neighborhood I was in was completely deserted. Maybe the people were taking siestas? I don't know. I sat down on the street corner to smoke my cigarette, and while I was taking a couple of really satisfying, deep drags of that full, rich, tobacco flavor, my mind turned to the match in my hand, and I contemplated the little gnarled piece of wood absentmindedly for a few moments.

Then I looked down and saw a crack in the pavement near my right foot, and I consciously decided to tuck that little match into that crack in the concrete. I thought to myself, No one will ever see it there.

And then I thought to myself, If no one ever sees this match, and nobody saw me put it there, and nobody knows about it except for me, what is the meaning of me hiding this match in this crack in the street in this little beach town outside of Caracas, Venezuela? Is there any meaning to this event?

And then I asked myself the big question: What is the meaning of my life?

A person's life is just like a match. It exists in a little box for a period of time. Then for a very short while it burns brightly. Then it is extinguished, or exhausts itself, and dies. And then it gets tucked into a little crack in the ground. That's it.

Perhaps you will have a tombstone, so you are arguing in your mind, Well I'll have a tombstone, so I'm not the same as the match because the match has no tombstone! Let's just consider this essay the metaphorical tombstone of the match—so your life and the match in the crack in Venezuela are exactly the same.

Then I thought to myself, Aha! But this match in the crack in the beach town in Venezuela does have meaning—it has meaning to **me**! I will never forget this moment, and I will never forget this match.

Of all the thousands of matches that I've lit and thrown away in my lifetime, that is the only one that has any meaning: that match in the crack in Venezuela. The rest of them were worthless, but that one revealed to me the meaning of life.

The meaning of life—and more importantly, the meaning of your life—is whatever you make it mean for you.

That match could have been like all the rest, but it wasn't. Because I made it mean something—to me, and now to you, and soon to hundreds of thousands (or millions) of people around the world.

That little match in the crack in Venezuela holds the key to the meaning of life! A little match!

For some people, the meaning of life is struggle.

For others, it is triumph over adversity.

Other people's lives are about justice. And others live for boredom.

Family. Friendship. Art. Love.

Work. Travel. People. Laughter.

Duty. Service. God.

Self.

Country.

Charity.

Religion.

Spirituality.

Physical fitness.

Disease.

You are living the exact life that you want. Remember—you would have changed it if you wanted something else. So this is the life you created for yourself, and these are the circumstances you've designed and orchestrated and starred in. This is your match and your beach town and your crack.

So what is the meaning of your life?

ACTION ITEM:

The meaning of my life is: _____

_____

_____

_____

DIG DEEP AND FIGURE THIS OUT NOW – FOR YOURSELF!

EXTRA CREDIT: Paste in a picture of the meaning of your life:

Week 49. Make Peace with Yourself & Your Higher Power

*"What all men are really after is some form
or perhaps only some formula of peace."*
–Joseph Conrad

It's time to let it all go now.

The struggle is over. The quest is over. All there is now is what there is.

You have had forty-eight complete weeks to go for the things you thought you wanted—to try as hard as you could to make them happen. Some of them came true; others didn't. Some things you got; some things you'll never get.

It's okay either way. Because it's time to let it all go.

If anything else comes through for you this year, then that's gravy. You've got a lot of momentum going, and stuff very well could happen—which is great—but now it's time to stop trying to do stuff. Now it's just time to be at peace.

This is what that's going to look like: you're going to stop making tons of phone calls trying to drum up business; you're going to stop sending out solicitations of any kind; you're going to stop going out raging and partying like it's 1999; you're going to slow it all way down.

This week you are going to take long walks by yourself on the beach, or in the woods, or in the mountains.

This week you are going to pray. Go to a church or a temple or any quiet and spiritual place, and just be alone with your thoughts and your dreams and your prayers.

Let everything external in the world go.

Just be inside yourself. Be with yourself. Be with your higher power.

Be still. Be satisfied. Be grateful.

Be alive.

Be, be, be. Just be enough.

Know that you are enough. Just the way you are. Just as you are.

Just you.

ACTION ITEMS: Each day this week, you are to sit and be enough for one hour. Go someplace different each day, and enjoy the peace of being you. Write down the different places.

1)

2)

3)

4)

5)

6)

7)

Week 50. Take Stock of Everything You Accomplished This Year

"It's been a good run, wouldn't you say?
You've made the most of every day.
But now it's too late.
It's too late, 'cause you're running out of time."
–Randy Jean

Do yourself a huge favor and listen to the song "The Last Year of Your Life" by Randy Jean. Click on this link, or type it into a web browser and take it in. http://web.me.com/clintarthur/Site/The_Last_Year_Of_Your_Life_-_Song_by_Randy_Jean.html

That song is all about you. It's about the past fifty weeks' experience that you've created for yourself. Yep, you did it.

I helped, but you made it happen. It's a tremendous accomplishment to undertake so much introspection, projection, manifestation, striving, dreaming, taking action, being courageous, pushing past your boundaries and fears, trying harder, staying up late, going to bed early—doing whatever it took for you to make it happen.

Bravo! Bravo for you!

Say "Bravo, me!" Go ahead, I'm waiting for you to say it. "Bravo ME!" You earned it.

Now I want you to take a look back at the marvelous year you created for yourself. Flip through the pages of this book; look at the photos in your camera, phone, computer, or scrapbook; read the writings, journals, notes in the margins, and whatever other memories you created for yourself.

I want you to spend the week enjoying the memories of this amazing year.

ACTION ITEMS: Write about the following subjects.

1) The most fun I had all year: _____
_____
_____

2) The scariest thing I did during this program: _____
_____
_____

3) The gutsiest thing I did during this program: _____
_____
_____

4) The best meal I ate during this program: _____
_____
_____

5) The most profound experience I had during this program: _____
_____
_____

6) The best trip I took during this program: _____
_____
_____

7) My fondest memory of the last year of my life: _____
_____
_____

8) The biggest lesson I learned from participating in this program: _____
_____
_____

Week 51. Experience True Freedom

"Even the longest day has its end."
–Irish Proverb

This week you are going to craft your own ritual death ceremony.

You are going to envision it; you are going to compile all the props and pieces of it; you are going to script it; you are going to get it ready in every possible way so that it has meaning and feels profound and resonant with your unique and custom circumstances.

This will be a somber time.

Contemplative.

Peaceful.

Respectful.

Slow.

Deliberate.

Mournful.

This is the preparation for the end of your life.

It should be custom just for your unique circumstances.

I want you to write a full CPR and agenda for this event. Take your time and be sure to gather all the items, people, and ideas you need to make this special for you.

Get everything ready by the end of this week, and then try to forget about it until the 365th day of The Last Year of Your Life. Then go for it!

*****

For the sake of giving you some ideas, this is some of what I have done in past years with prior program participants:

The ritual starts at high noon, and we begin with a game. The exact game is irrelevant, as any game will do. The key point is that there is competition, and whenever one side scores a point, the game stops and the person who was scored upon prepares to "die." Before they exit the playing field, they have to declare how they would have lived their life differently.

For example, when I got eliminated, I stood still and screamed, "My life is over, and if I had it to live all over again, I would have called or texted my daughter every day."

Everyone kept playing until only one participant remained, and this person was the winner of the game. They still had to declare what they would have done differently, just like everyone else.

Then we moved to the sacred space and cleansed the air with burning sage.

And then we brought out the lamb.

As I held it in my arms, the lamb became remarkably calm and docile. All the participants put their hands on the lamb and petted it. A Jewish participant in the event led us in a prayer ceremony as we each prayed for the lamb and thanked it for its sacrifice on our behalf.

Then a Native American shaman joined us in our circle and instructed me to put the lamb on the ground. As it stood there, he embraced it in the fold of his arms and he covered it with the wing of an eagle—which was one of his personal ceremonial artifacts—as he prayed over it in his Native American language.

When the shaman finished praying over the lamb, he nodded to me and I took control over the animal again. I stood over the lamb, with it standing between my legs, and I asked every person in the circle to gently put a hand on the lamb and hold it.

Then I unsheathed a large and very sharp hunting knife and slit a quick and thorough cut across the lamb's neck, severing its arteries and cutting all the way deep to its spine, as is the tradition in Kosher and Halal slaughter rituals.

The animal never uttered a sound as it bled out into a metal pail we had placed before it to collect the blood.

This was one of the most disturbing things I've ever done in my life. But it also connected me to the ancient ritual of slaughtering a lamb for sacrifice and feasting, which is a tradition that has gone on in the many cultures of our species since time immemorial.

While some of the participants dressed the animal and prepared it for the feast, others prepared a roaring fire.

With those elements of the ritual in place, we cracked open a cold bottle of champagne and toasted to the lamb that had sacrificed its life for us. Then we cut up its heart into little pieces and ate a raw slice of lamb heart.

By this point it started getting dark. The participants stuffed the lamb with lemons, garlic, and onions, then slathered it with butter and olive oil—all according to traditional Greek feasting traditions. Then they placed it on a spit and began to slowly roast it over the hot coals in the fire. We placed big pans of potatoes, sprinkled with wild rosemary leaves and onions, on the coals beneath the lamb and allowed its juices to drip into the pans as the spit was kept slowly and constantly turning.

During the cooking, we began the next phase of ritual: stories.

I instructed the participants that we would go around the circle, and every person would tell one story. The rules were simple: it had to be a true story that you personally had either witnessed or participated in yourself. The goal of this ritual was to look back over your life and to share with everyone the very best story that you had ever been a part of—the most intense, the most amazing, the most horrible, the most fun, the scariest, the most meaningful —whatever story you wanted to tell, as long as it was your best story. When each person finished their story, they would say, "Top that!" and the next person would try to top it with something even more incredible.

One person told about when they were a paramedic and walked into a garage to find a woman strung up from the rafters with a bullet hole in her head.

Another participant told about the time when he came home and found his wife, the mother of their child, hanging dead in the bathroom—a suicide.

I told the story of the birth of my daughter—how the labor had begun in the afternoon as "false labor," and by eleven o'clock that night we were in the hospital and I was running all around Cedars Sinai looking for our obstetrician because he was supposedly in the building. I was running around and around all frantic, and I actually got dizzy.

They gave my daughter's mother a drug to induce the labor, and we spent all night together watching Beavis & Butt-head on MTV while the contractions increased. Still, by dawn the birth had not progressed, and the doctor determined the umbilical cord was wrapped around my daughter's neck.

At 8 a.m. I sat all alone in the hallway outside an operating room while a team of medical professionals prepared to perform an emergency c-section. I prayed to God, one of the very, very few times in my life when I asked for his help, and I pleaded for my daughter and her mother to be alright.

A nurse came and brought me into the operating theater, and the doctor told me to stand at the mother's head and comfort her. I held her hand while I watched the doctor and his assisting physician yank open the incision in her belly. The doctor was on one side of the operating table, his assistant was on the other; they had their fingers in the little incision, then the doctor said, "One, two, three!" and they both leaned back and yanked the hole open wide in her belly.

Then the doctor looked inside, reached his hand in, and pulled my daughter out into the big bad world. He said, "Your daughter is being born now."

As he held her high so we could see, she opened her eyes and blinked against the bright lights of the operating room. Her hair was thick and black and wet from amniotic fluid.

It was quiet and reverential in the operating room while she took her first looks at the new world around her. Then the doctor smacked her on the butt and she started crying. A nurse took her to a side table and started cleaning her up, and a moment later the doctor said, "Daddy, why don't you go be with your daughter."

I walked over to my newborn child and saw her crying on the steel table. I took her little hand in mine and said, "Don't cry, Cali. Everything is alright."

She immediately stopped crying at the sound of my voice and looked at me.

She knew who I was. She knew me by the sound of my voice.

*****

When everyone had told their story, we feasted. The lamb and vegetables were delicious, and unlike any other food I'd ever eaten. I was hardly hungry, but out of respect for the food and for the animal who had given up its life, I ate everything.

After dinner, a few of the participants performed songs that they had written for the occasion, and the music was sweet and sad and beautiful and melancholy.

After the performances, we had our last dessert: simple s'mores made of Hershey bars, graham crackers, and marshmallows.

Then it was time to clean up. When all the dishes had been washed and the campsite put in order, we changed into ceremonial robes which had been purchased just for this occasion.

I had everyone reassemble around the campfire. I distributed a cup of liquid to each person and informed them, "This is the drink that will end your life."

Everyone drank their drink, and I led us to the ceremonial lodge. As each person stood at the entrance to the lodge, they held their obituary (which they had written beforehand and brought to the event) and I looked them in the eyes and said, "Your life is over. Now (person's name) is dead."

As they crawled through the small flap opening into the ceremonial lodge, they each said, "My life is over. (Their name) is dead."

I was the last person to enter the lodge, and before I did, I got down on my hands and knees and said, "My life is over. Clint Arthur is dead."

Inside the lodge it was pitch–black darkness. The air was stagnant, and it was already beginning to get humid.

The participants were arrayed around a central pit dug into the floor of the lodge, and they were all sitting on Native American blankets, much like the ones found in Mexico.

I had a tiny flashlight with me, and I turned it on to illuminate my obituary. I said, "This is the obituary of Clint Arthur." Then I read my obituary aloud.

When I finished reading my obituary, I handed the flashlight to the person next to me, and I laid down flat on the ground.

As we each read our obituaries, one by one, some people were crying, some people were silent, and one by one the people faded out into the nothingness of eternal slumber.

ACTION ITEM:

Create your own death ritual.

Participants:

Opening event: (something fun and physical)

Ritual "sacrifice":

Feast:

Closing ritual:

"Death sacrament":

Death ritual:

TO PURCHASE THE OFFICIAL CLINT ARTHUR DEATH RITUAL SACRAMENT, go to www.TheLastYearOfYourLife.com/The_Last_Year_Of_Your_Life/Sacrament.html

Week 52. Create A Clean Slate For The Rest Of Your Life

"He not busy being born is busy dying."
–Bob Dylan

During the night, our Native American shaman and his assistant prepared a fire and heated ceremonial stones until they were glowing red with intense heat.

Some time before the dawn, the shaman crawled into the ceremonial lodge. He started to receive the stones from his assistant and place them in the pit which had been dug into the center of the floor. They used special ceremonial antlers to transfer the rocks from the fire outside into the pit; they each had a set of this special tool, and they passed the burning stones between them quite deftly.

Gradually everyone awoke from their death sleep into this state of limbo, and when the shaman had satisfied himself as to the amount of rocks in the pit, his assistant joined us inside the lodge and they began the chanting.

Native American chanting is very primal, and although nobody else besides the shaman was a Native American, many people joined in on the chanting.

I don't know or remember what was said or what we prayed for, but it was hot as anything I'd ever experienced, and soon I was drenched with sweat and my robes were soaked through.

Abruptly the chanting came to an end and the shaman crawled out into the dawning sunlight, followed by his assistant. Only the participants and I remained in the lodge.

I said, "The person nearest the door is going to go first. When you crawl into the threshold, I want you to pause in the doorway and say 'My name is—whatever your name is—and today is the first day of my new life.' One by one."

That's what we did.

One at a time, each person crawled to the doorway, paused, said the mantra, and was reborn, until at last it was my turn. I crawled all around the pit in the center of the circle; I paused in the threshold and, blinking against the bright light of the sunrise, I said, "My name is Clint Arthur, and today is the first day of my new life."

We stood in a circle around the campfire, and each person drank their own bottle of sweet–sweet precious water. No water ever tasted so good.

The shaman said a few words, then each person expressed their gratitude to be alive, and then we feasted to break our fast. The feast was raw oysters with fresh lemon squeezes, croissants, and bottles of Starbucks iced Frappuccinos. What a feast!

*****

Now you are going to design your own rebirth ritual and ceremony. I suggest you include a feast at the end to break your fast.

All celebrations, in my humble opinion, should include feasting.

Yours doesn't have to look like mine or ours. I've only written mine up to use as an illustration for what is possible, and hopefully to inspire you to come up with something meaningful of your own.

If you can work in tandem with a spiritual leader to design this experience with you, I would highly advise it. This is magic we're invoking here. Human beings have been pursuing the alchemy of rituals and ceremonies for hundreds of thousands of years, and the ancient wisdom is more alive today than you would imagine.

Go out there and make magic come alive in your life.

PART 3

Creating a Vision & Plan For
Your Ideal Life in Five Years' Time

"Dream lofty dreams, and as you dream, so shall you become.
Your vision is the promise of what you shall one day be;
your ideal is the prophecy of what you shall at last unveil."
–James Allen

Immediately after your ritual rebirth and breakfast feast, I want you to use your heightened state and awareness to create a brilliant future for yourself —more exciting and inspirational than anything you've ever lived.

I want you to envision what your ideal life would look like five years in the future. Imagine that you have exactly the house you've always wanted, the exact car, the job you've always dreamed of, the spouse or significant other who inspires you, the toys, the skills, the geographic location—whatever you truly, in your heart of hearts, want or need in order to be living the life of your dreams.

Write it down. In as much detail as you possibly can, write it all down. Take thirty minutes and do it now.

My Ideal Life in Five Years' Time:_____

_____

_____

_____

_____

_____

_____

_____

_____

_____

_____

_____

_____
_____
_____
_____
_____
_____
_____
_____
_____
_____
_____
_____
_____
_____
_____
_____
_____
_____
_____
_____
_____
_____
_____
_____
_____
_____

Sign: Date:

Congratulations!

"All our dreams can come true...
if we have the courage to pursue them."
–Walt Disney

You have now graduated from The Last Year of Your Life Program.

Your old life has gone out with a bang! Your new, ideal life awaits you.

Five years from now I want you to be living in that dream house (or houses), driving the car you've always wanted, doing the work you were put on this Earth to do, sharing your precious existence with the people you want to share it with, and living every aspect of the life you dreamed you could one day live.

That is the special gift of The Last Year of Your Life. I hope you see now that it really was The Last Year of Your Life. Now you are beginning the first year of your New Life.

Your New Life is the life of your dreams.

Enjoy!

With much love,

I will always be your humble, fellow adventurer,

Other Books by Clint Arthur

What They Teach You At The Wharton Business School

The Income Doubler: Double Your Income In 180 Days Or Less

Free Your Love Now

For more information visit...

www.FreeNewPower.com

www.TheIncomeDoubler.com

www.TheLastYearOfYourLife.com

For The Best Butter On Earth visit www.FiveStarButter.com

Made in the USA
Lexington, KY
29 December 2011